XCOM 2
FACTIONS

Written by Kevin J. Anderson

Illustrated by Michael Penick

Colors by Juanma Aguilera

Special Thanks to Will Rosado

INSIGHT COMICS

San Rafael, California

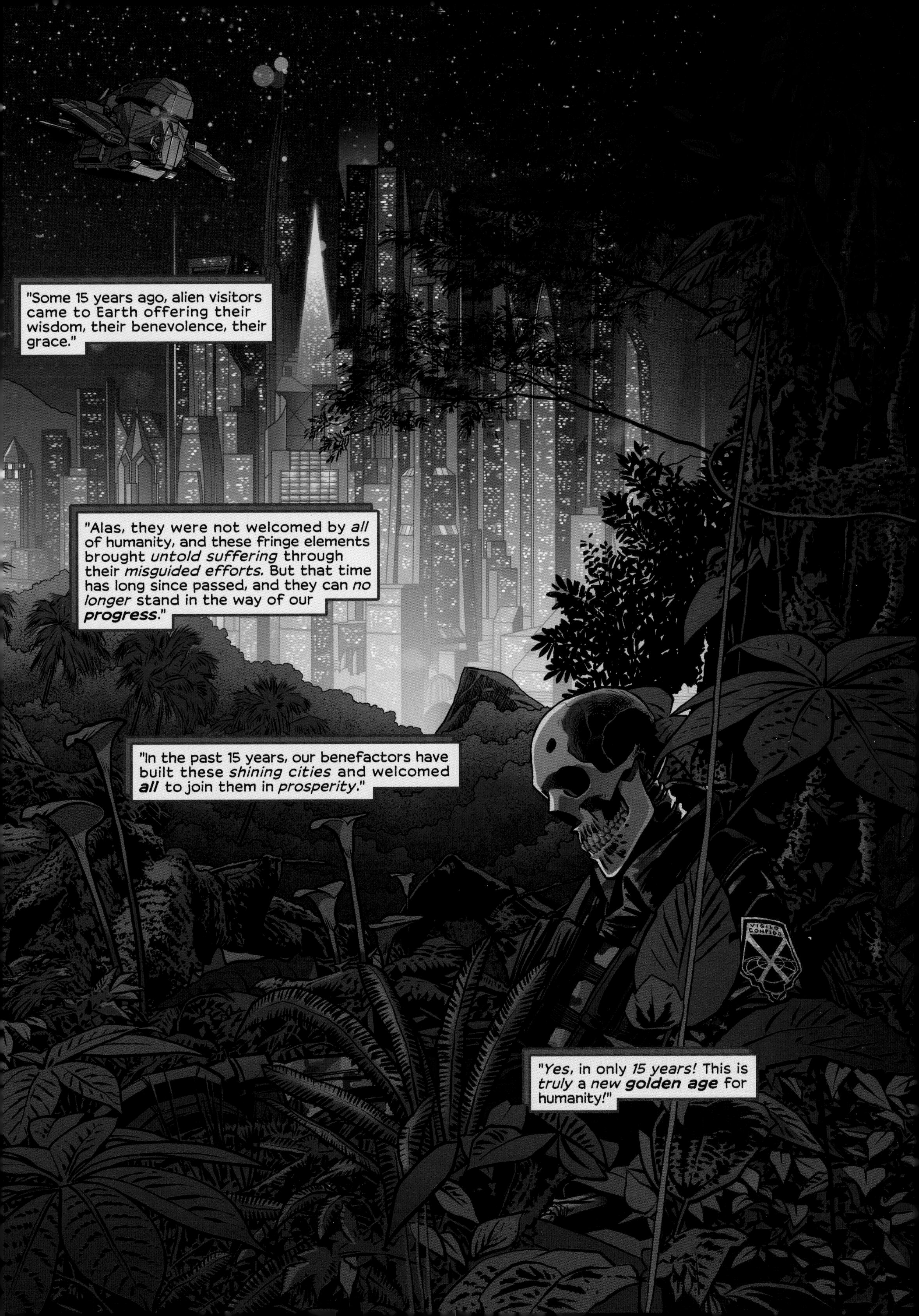
"Some 15 years ago, alien visitors came to Earth offering their wisdom, their benevolence, their grace."
"Alas, they were not welcomed by *all* of humanity, and these fringe elements brought *untold suffering* through their *misguided efforts.* But that time has long since passed, and they can *no longer* stand in the way of our ***progress***."
"In the past 15 years, our benefactors have built these *shining cities* and welcomed ***all*** to join them in *prosperity*."
VIGILO CONFIDO
"*Yes*, in only *15 years!* This is *truly* a *new* **golden age** for humanity!"

After decades of *violence*, *poverty*, and *sickness*, the world has *finally* been *saved*.

The world has ended, the world we *used to know*. 15 years might as well be an *eternity*.

"Thanks to the aliens, **ADVENT** cities offer *shelter*, *security*, and a *purpose* for *all* people--all those who choose to *accept* the gift of *hope*, *help*, and *prosperity*."

BUILDING A BRIGHTER
TOGETHER

The oceans, the cities, the landscape... all *devastated* by the invaders.

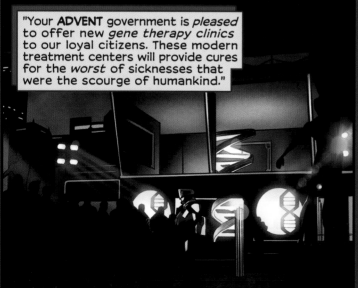

"Your **ADVENT** government is *pleased* to offer new *gene therapy* clinics to our loyal citizens. These modern treatment centers will provide cures for the *worst* of sicknesses that were the scourge of humankind."

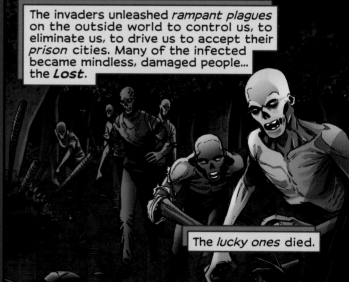

The invaders unleashed *rampant plagues* on the outside world to control us, to eliminate us, to drive us to accept their *prison* cities. Many of the infected became mindless, damaged people... the *Lost*.

The *lucky ones* died.

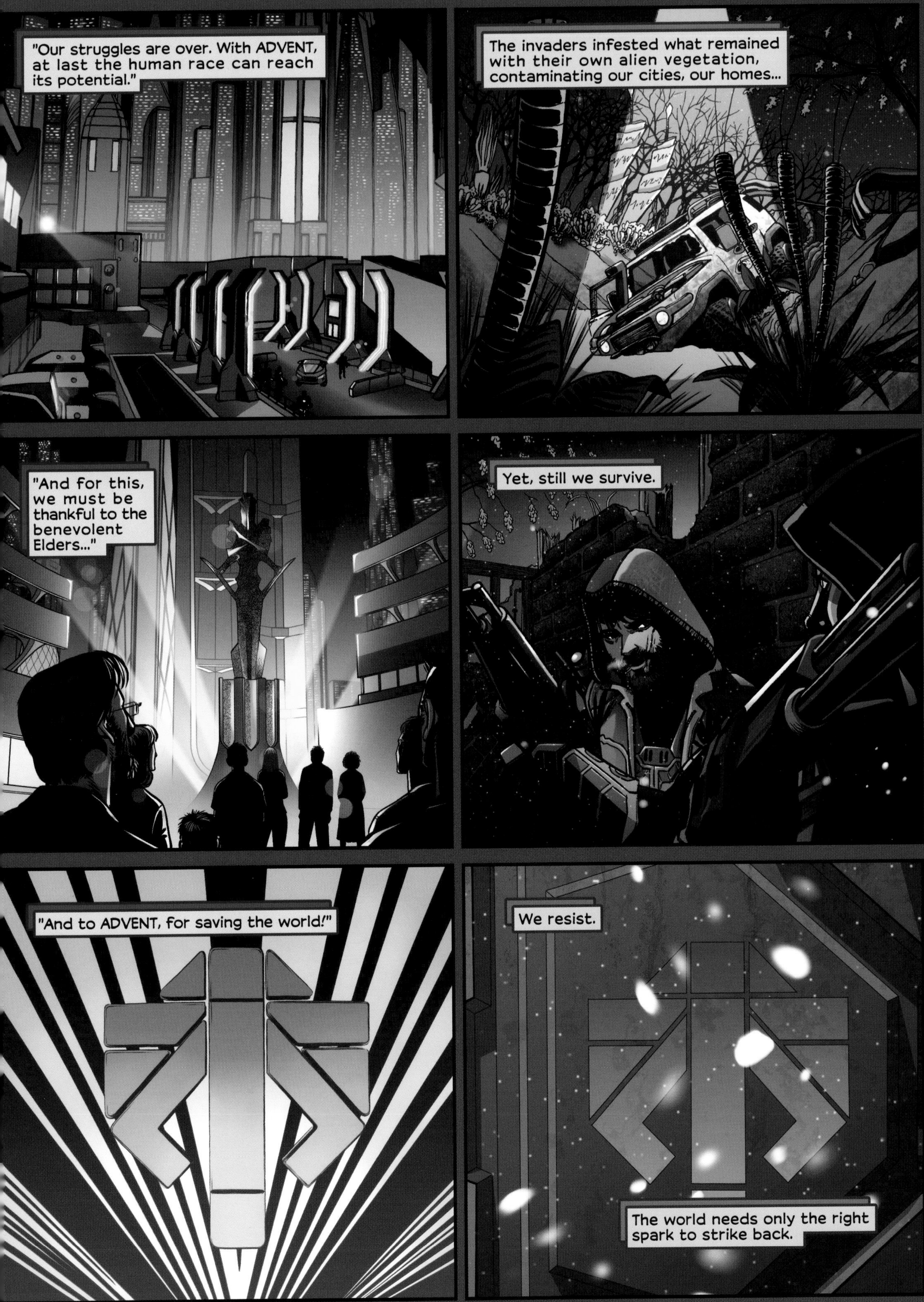
"Our struggles are over. With ADVENT, at last the human race can reach its potential."
The invaders infested what remained with their own alien vegetation, contaminating our cities, our homes...
"And for this, we must be thankful to the benevolent Elders..."
Yet, still we survive.
"And to ADVENT, for saving the world!"
We resist.
The world needs only the right spark to strike back.

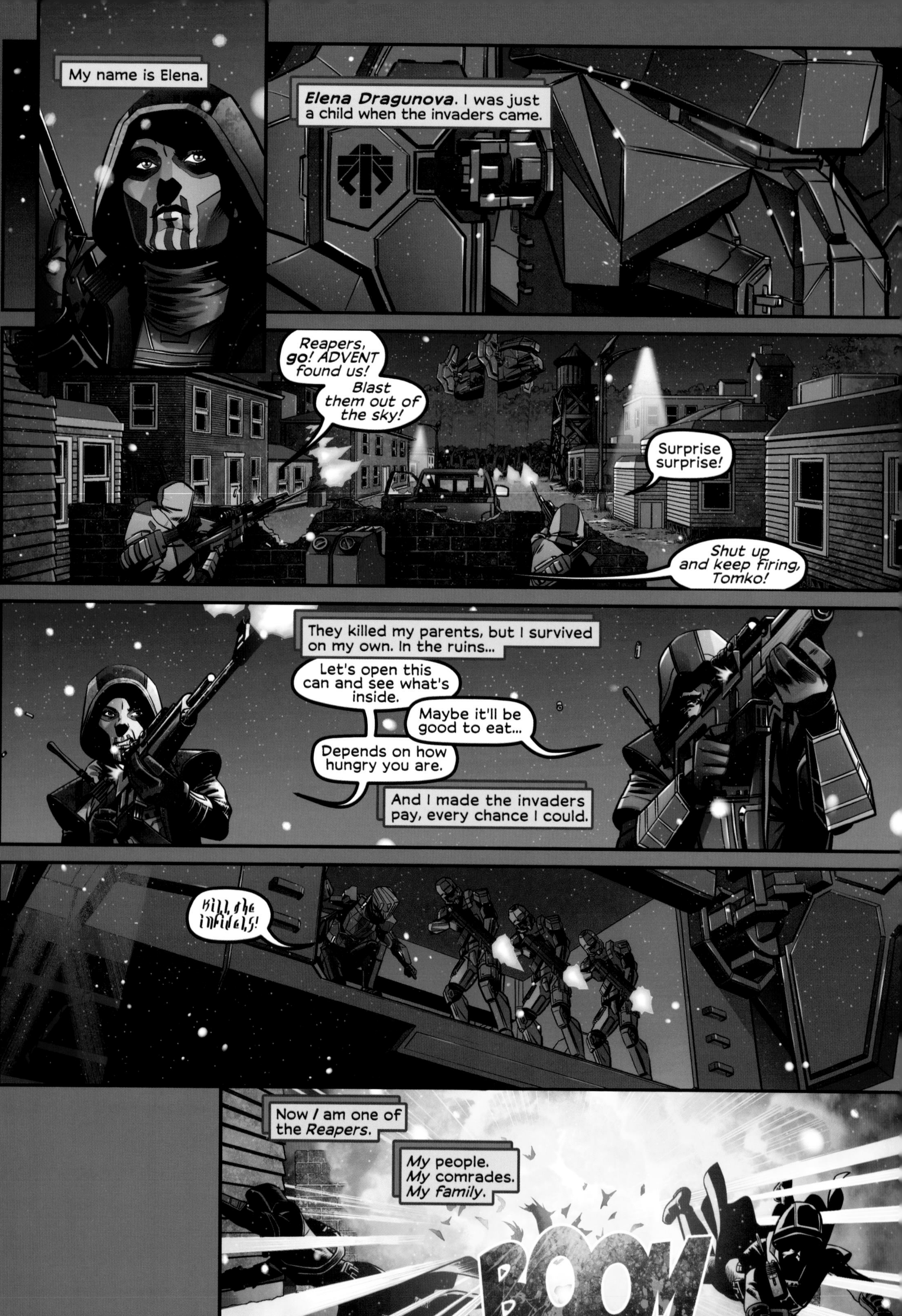

My name is Elena.
Elena Dragunova. I was just a child when the invaders came.
Reapers, **go**! ADVENT found us! Blast them out of the sky!
Surprise surprise!
Shut up and keep firing, Tomko!
They killed my parents, but I survived on my own. In the ruins...
Let's open this can and see what's inside.
Maybe it'll be good to eat...
Depends on how hungry you are.
And I made the invaders pay, every chance I could.
Kill the infidels!
Now *I* am one of the *Reapers*.
My people. *My* comrades. *My family*.
BOOM

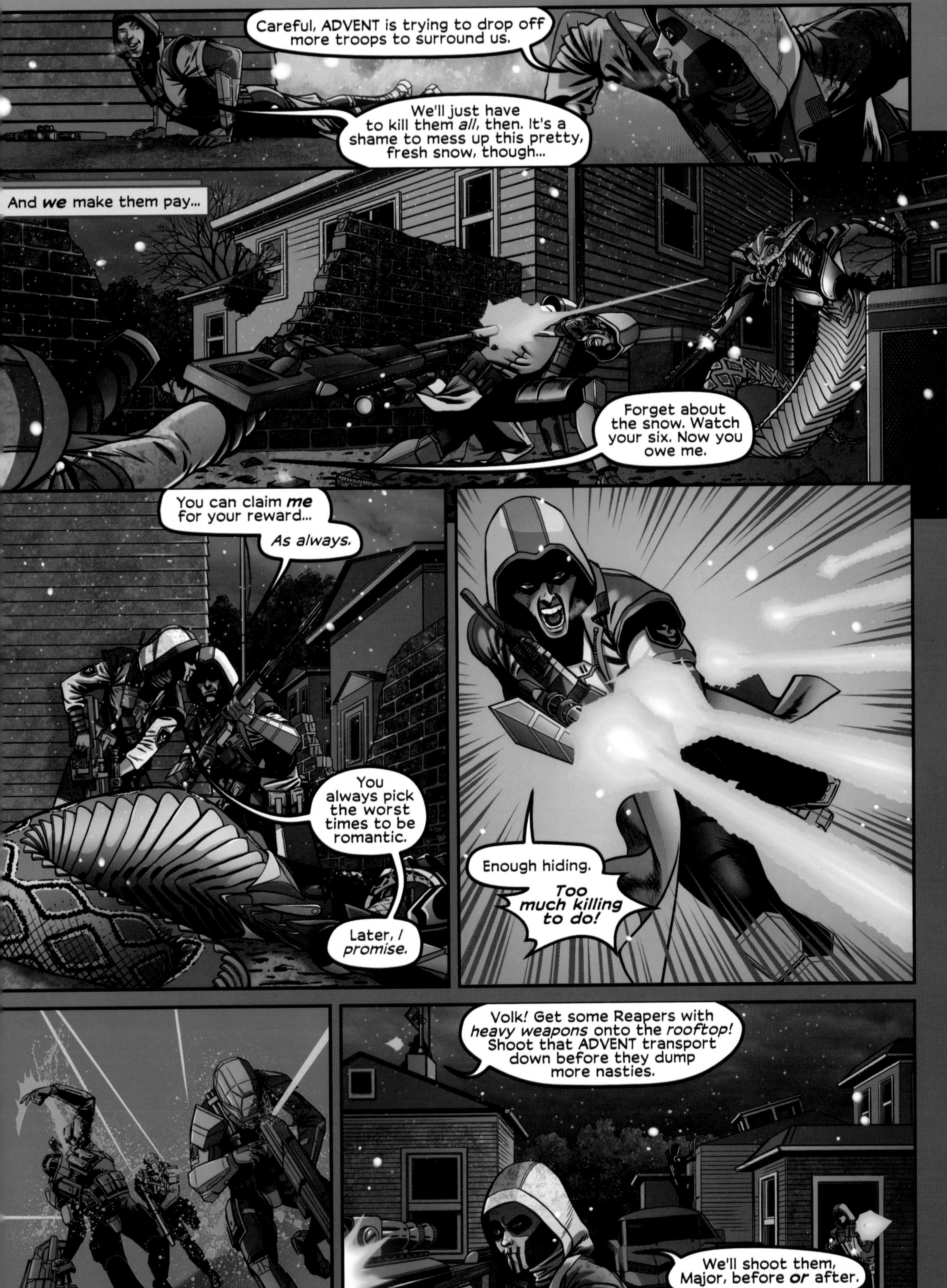
Careful, ADVENT is trying to drop off more troops to surround us.
We'll just have to kill them *all*, then. It's a shame to mess up this pretty, fresh snow, though...
And **we** make them pay...
Forget about the snow. Watch your six. Now you owe me.
You can claim ***me*** for your reward...
As always.
You always pick the worst times to be romantic.
Later, *I promise.*
Enough hiding.
Too much killing to do!
Volk! Get some Reapers with *heavy weapons* onto the *rooftop!* Shoot that ADVENT transport down before they dump more nasties.
We'll shoot them, Major, before ***or*** after.

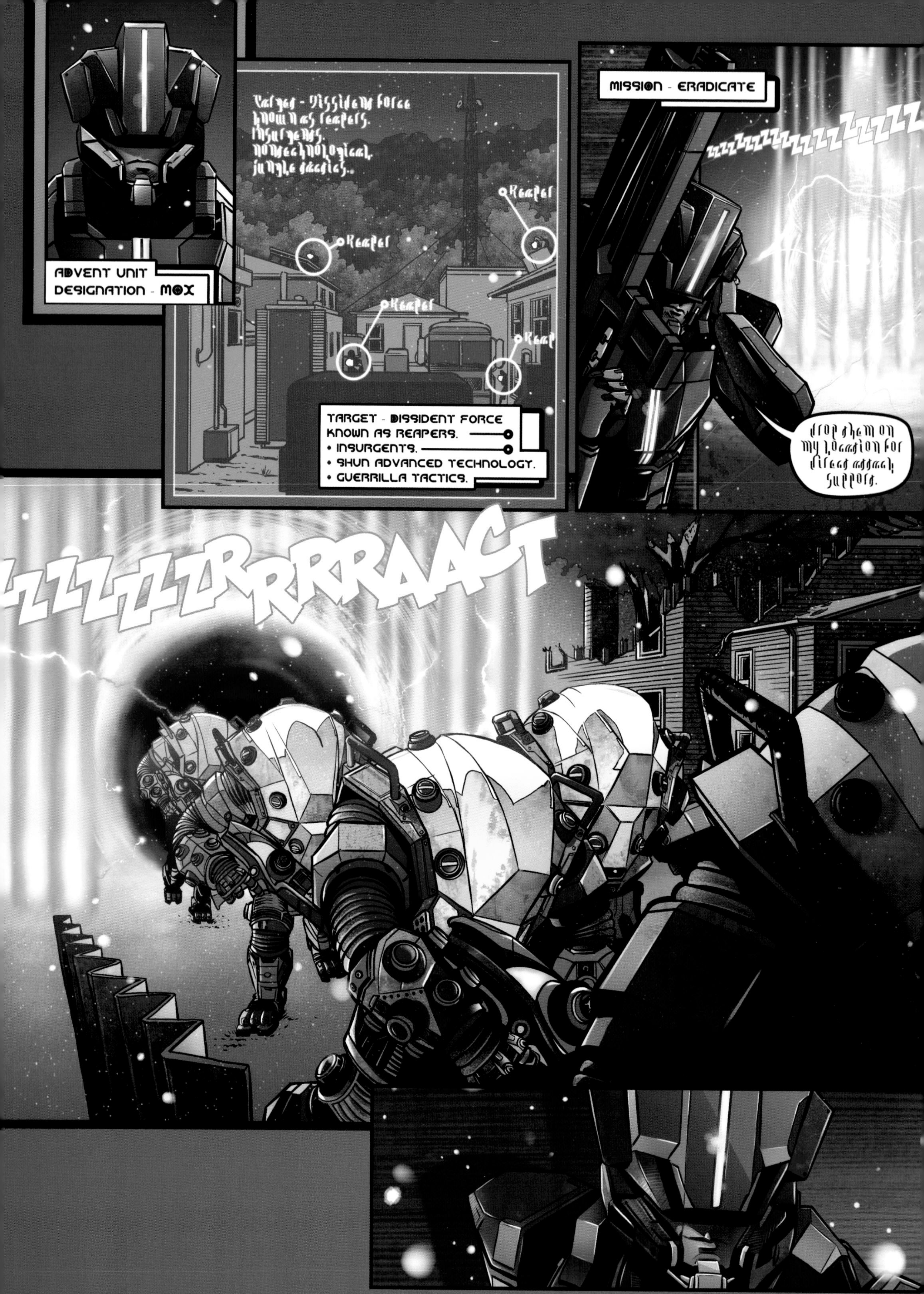
ADVENT UNIT
DESIGNATION - MOX
TARGET - DISSIDENT FORCE
KNOWN AS REAPERS.
• INSURGENTS.
• SHUN ADVANCED TECHNOLOGY.
• GUERRILLA TACTICS.
MISSION - ERADICATE
ZZZZZZZZZZZZZZZZZZZZZ
ZZZZZZZRRRRAACT

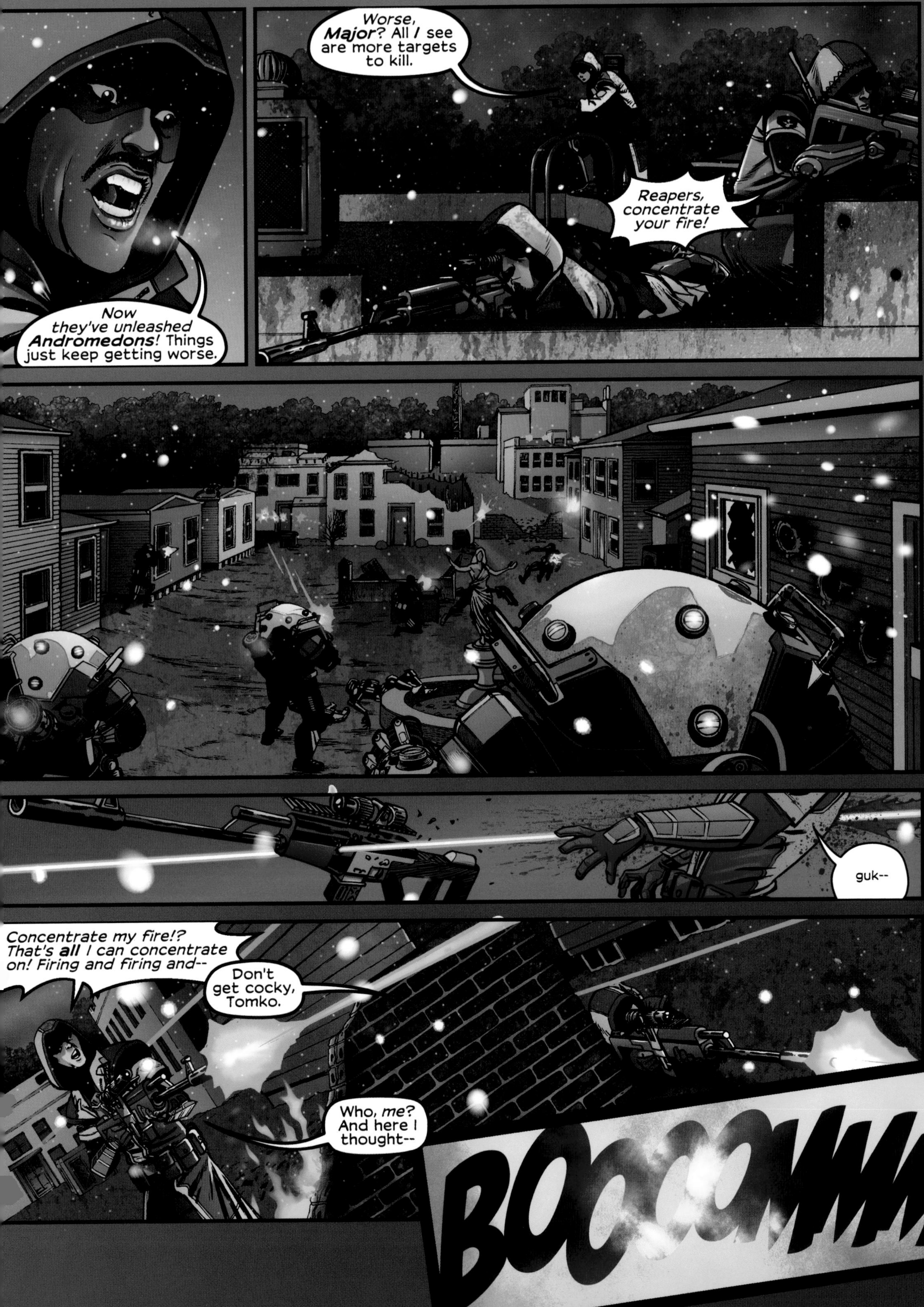
Now they've unleashed Andromedons! Things just keep getting worse.
Worse, Major? All I see are more targets to kill.
Reapers, concentrate your fire!
guk--
Concentrate my fire!? That's all I can concentrate on! Firing and firing and--
Don't get cocky, Tomko.
Who, me? And here I thought--
BOOOMM

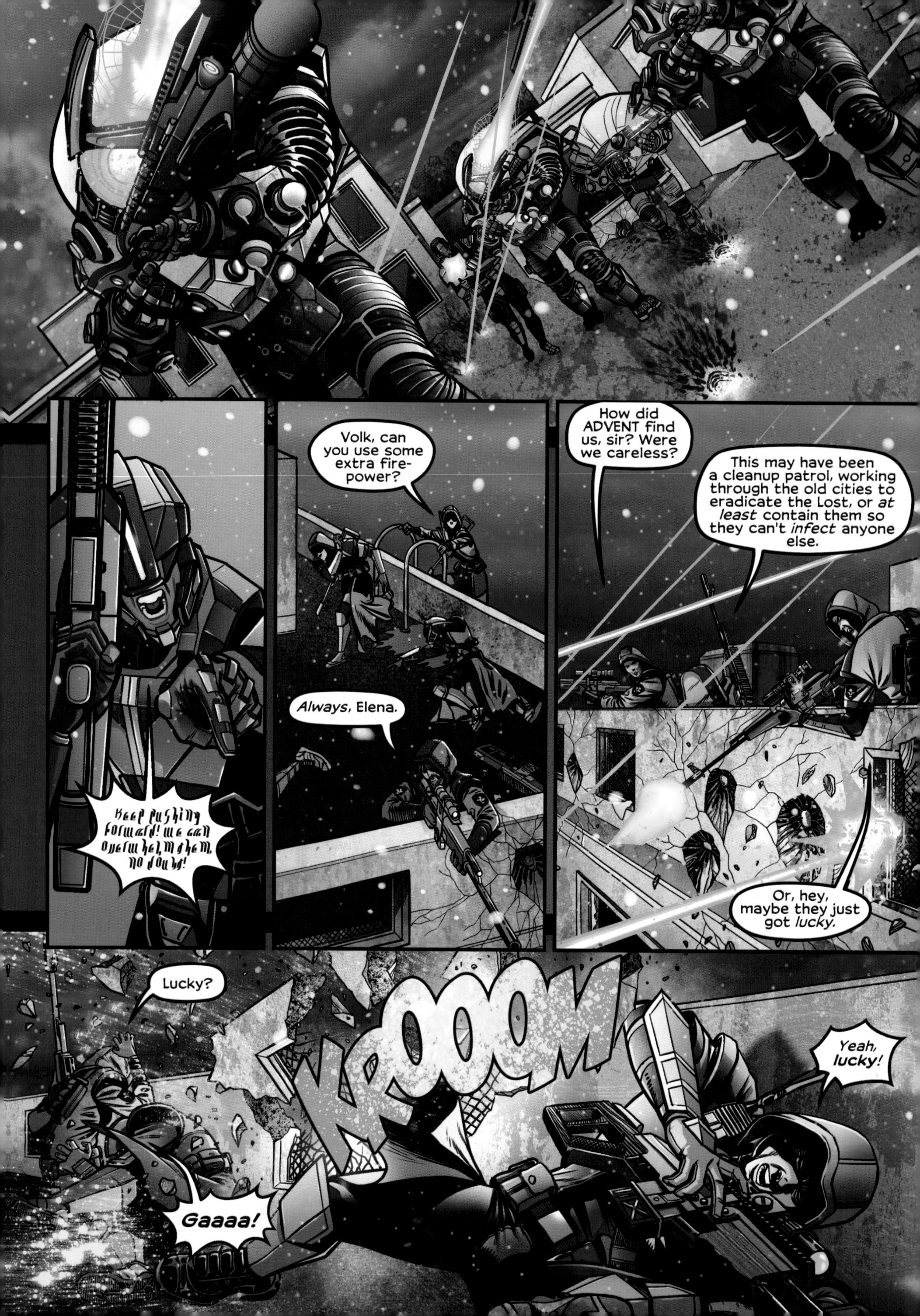

Keep pushing forward! We can overwhelm them, no doubt!
Volk, can you use some extra fire-power?
Always, Elena.
How did ADVENT find us, sir? Were we careless?
This may have been a cleanup patrol, working through the old cities to eradicate the Lost, or *at least* contain them so they can't *infect* anyone else.
Or, hey, maybe they just got *lucky*.
Lucky?
KROOOM
Yeah, ***lucky!***
Gaaaa!

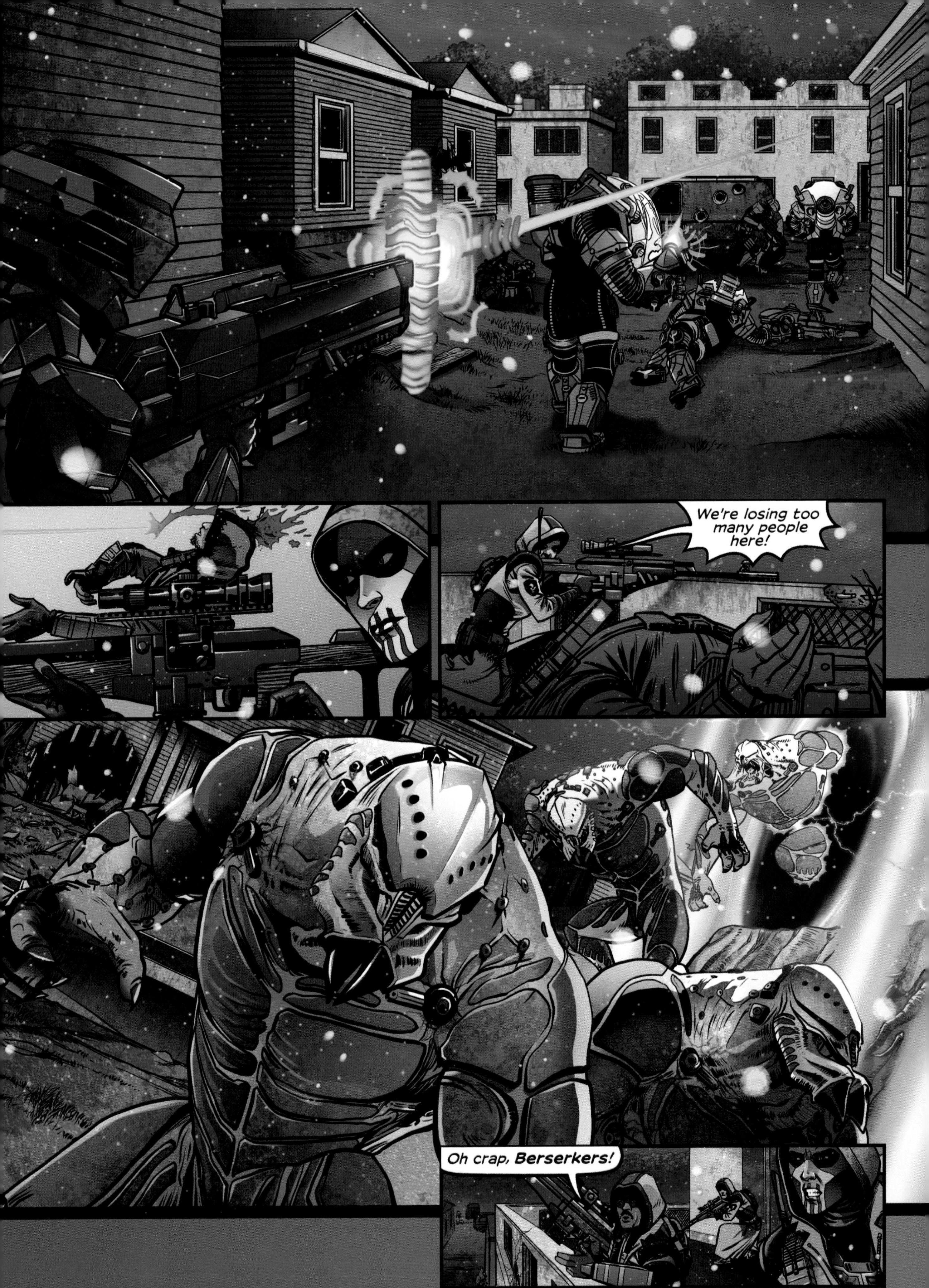
We're losing too many people here!
Oh crap, **Berserkers!**

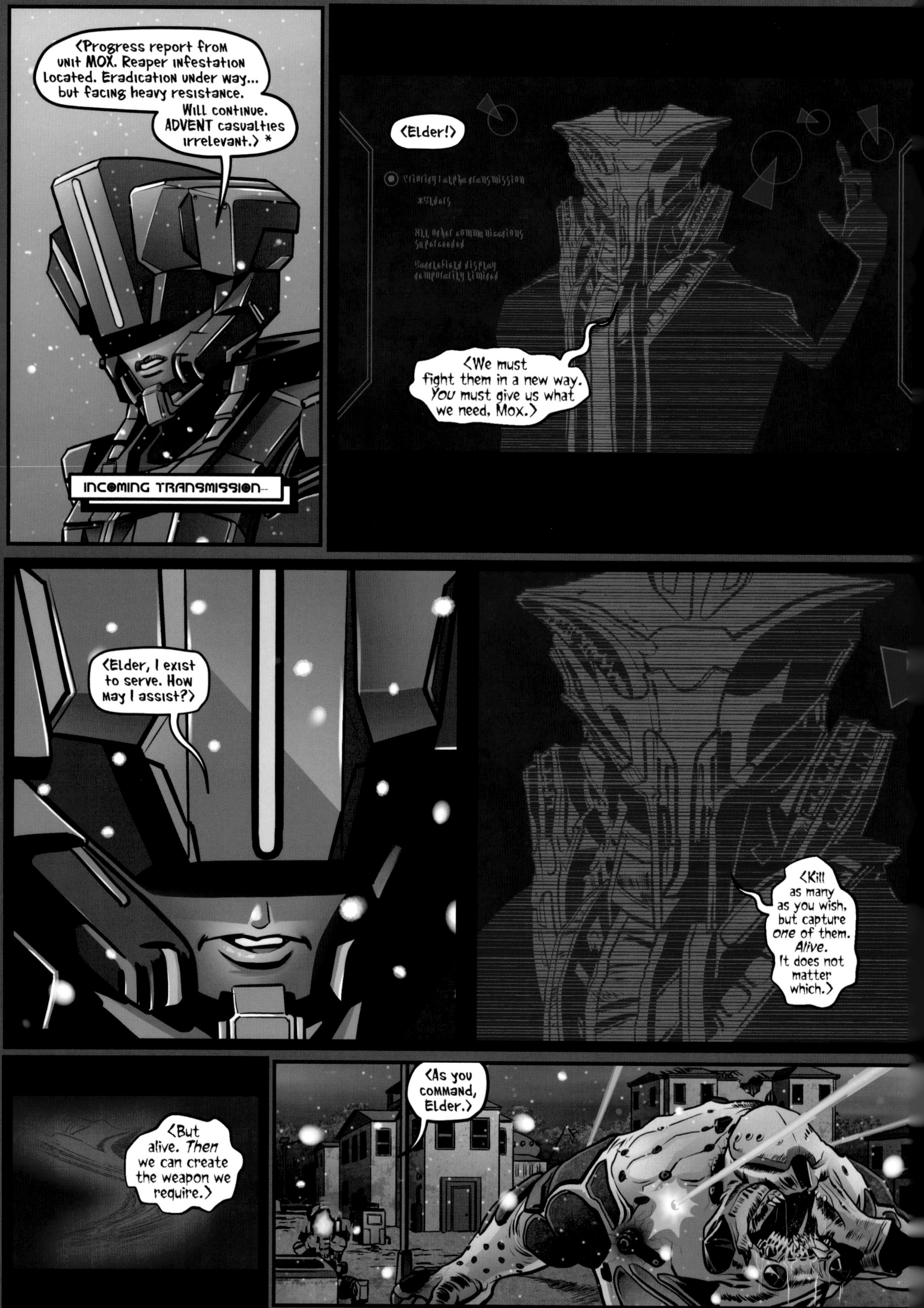

<Progress report from unit MOX. Reaper infestation located. Eradication under way... but facing heavy resistance.
Will continue. ADVENT casualties irrelevant.> *
INCOMING TRANSMISSION
<Elder!>
<We must fight them in a new way. *You* must give us what we need, Mox.>
<Elder, I exist to serve. How may I assist?>
<Kill as many as you wish, but capture *one* of them. *Alive*. It does not matter which.>
<But alive. *Then* we can create the weapon we require.>
<As you command, Elder.>

* Translated from ADV

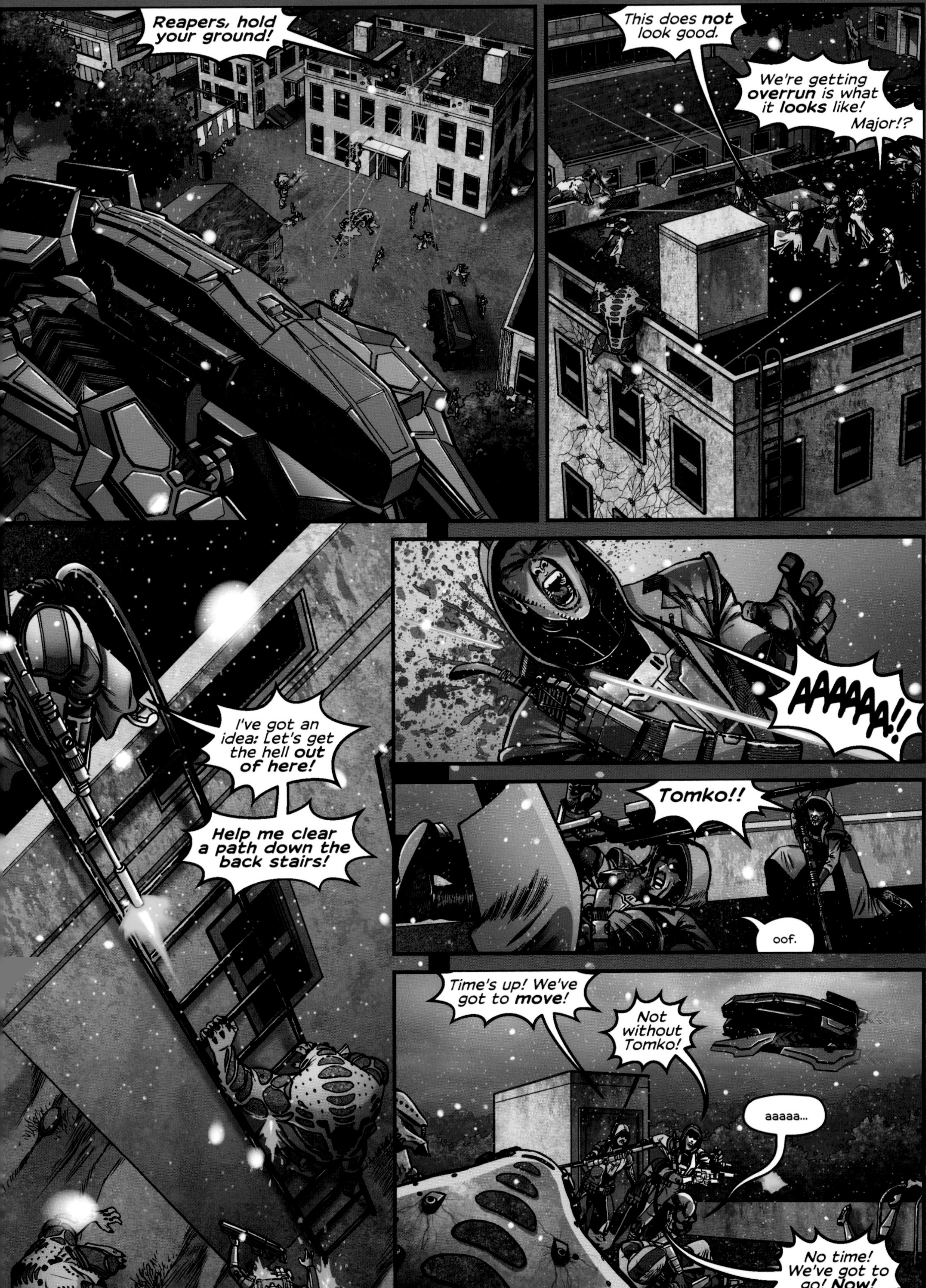
Reapers, hold your ground!
This does not look good.
We're getting overrun is what it looks like!
Major!?
I've got an idea: Let's get the hell out of here!
Help me clear a path down the back stairs!
AAAAAA!!
Tomko!!
oof.
Time's up! We've got to move!
Not without Tomko!
aaaaa...
No time! We've got to go! Now!

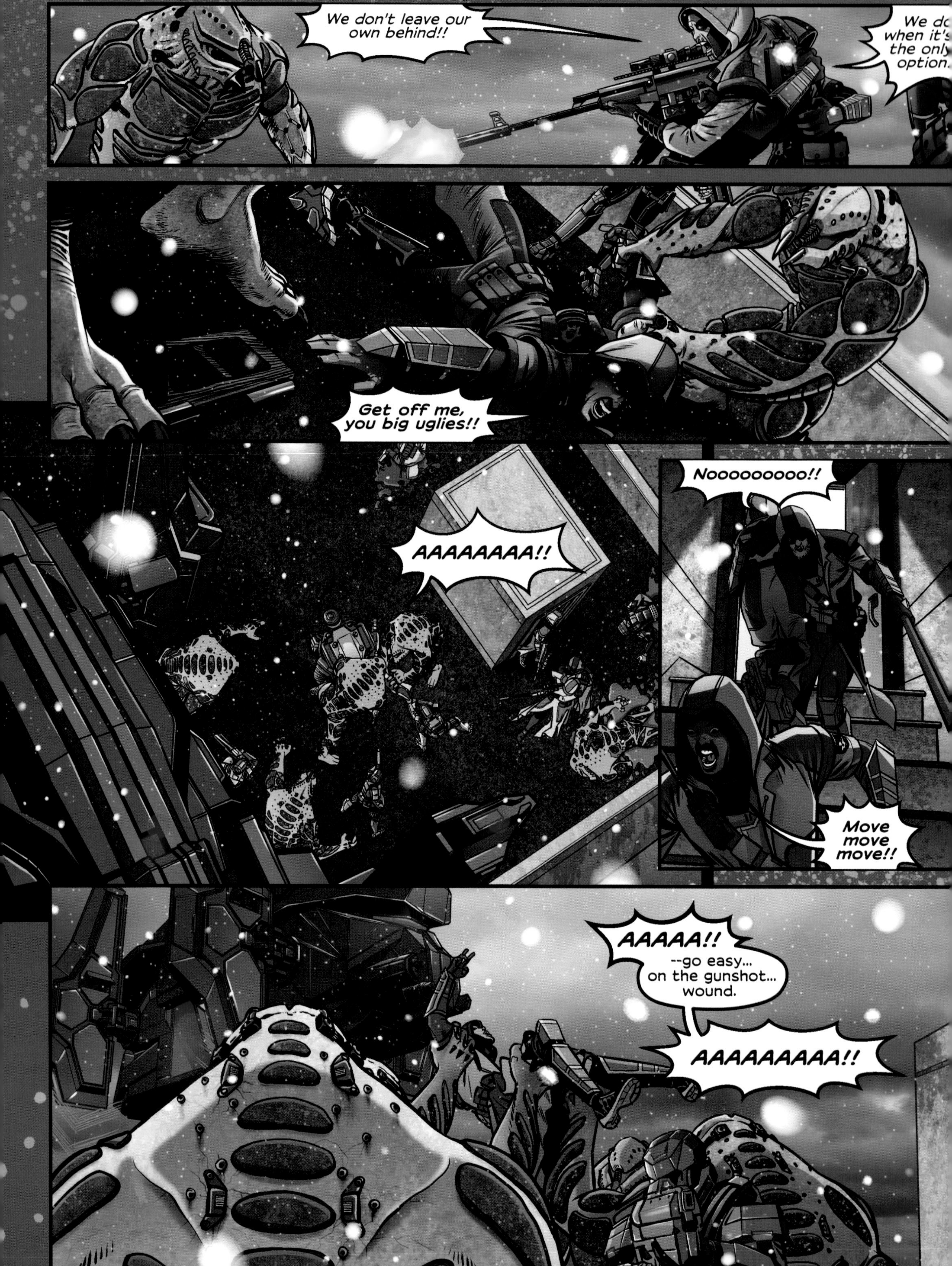

We don't leave our own behind!!
We do when it's the only option.
Get off me, you big uglies!!
AAAAAAAA!!
Noooooooooo!!
Move move move!!
AAAAA!! --go easy... on the gunshot... wound.
AAAAAAAAAA!!

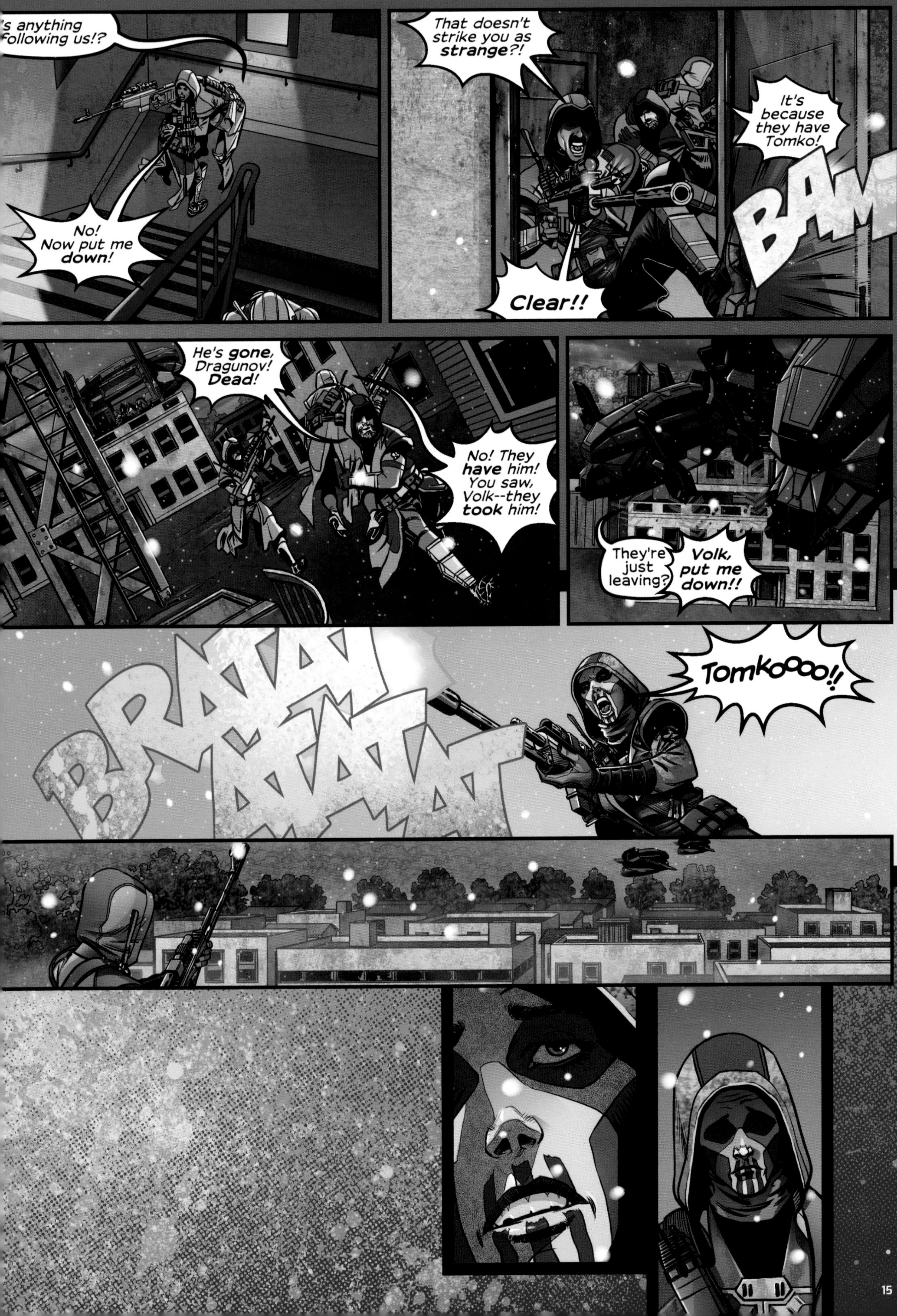
's anything following us!?
No! Now put me down!
That doesn't strike you as strange?!
It's because they have Tomko!
Clear!!
BAM
He's gone, Dragunov! Dead!
No! They have him! You saw, Volk--they took him!
They're just leaving?
Volk, put me down!!
Tomkoooo!!

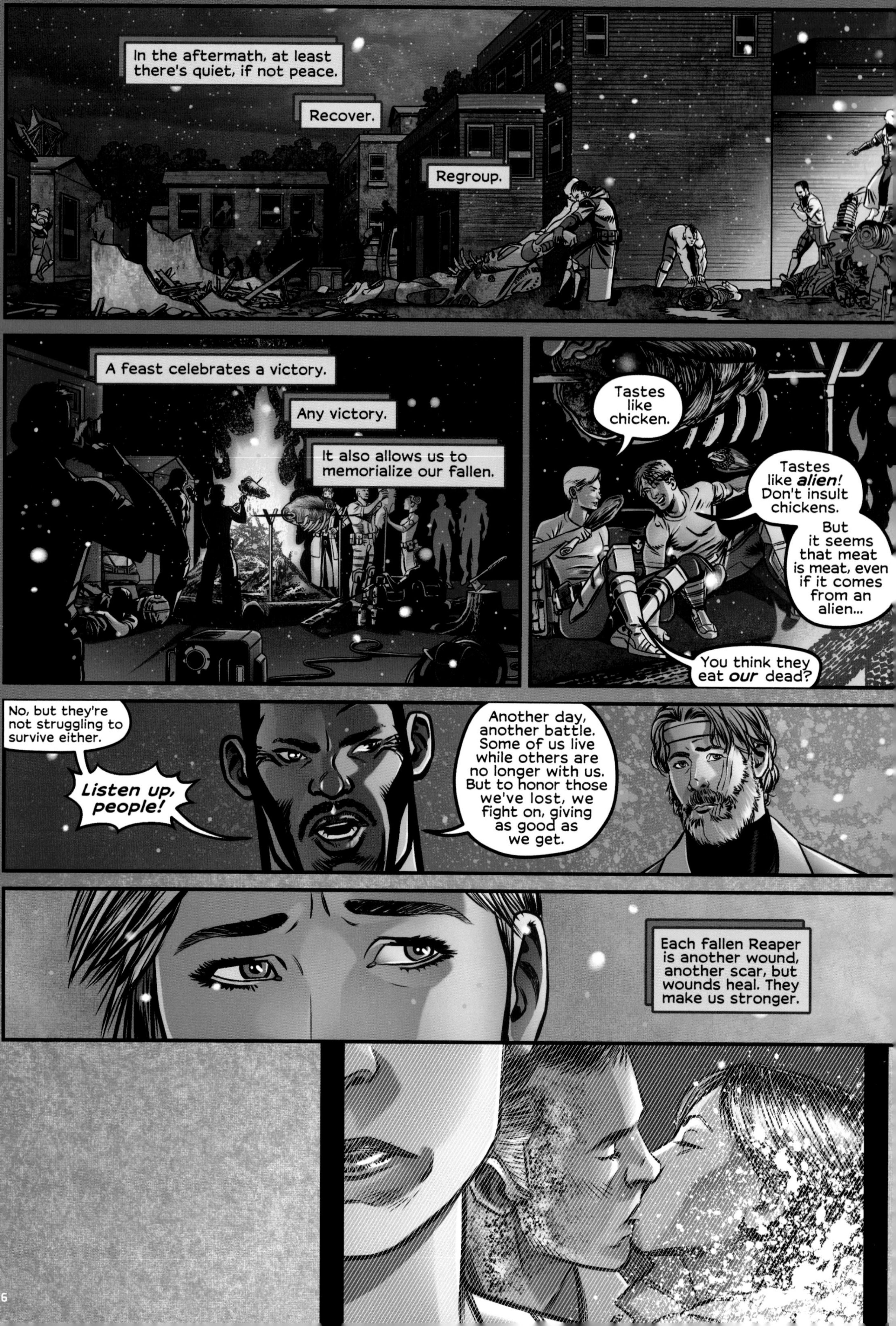

In the aftermath, at least there's quiet, if not peace.
Recover.
Regroup.
A feast celebrates a victory.
Any victory.
It also allows us to memorialize our fallen.
Tastes like chicken.
Tastes like *alien*! Don't insult chickens.
But it seems that meat is meat, even if it comes from an alien...
You think they eat *our* dead?
No, but they're not struggling to survive either.
Listen up, people!
Another day, another battle. Some of us live while others are no longer with us. But to honor those we've lost, we fight on, giving as good as we get.
Each fallen Reaper is another wound, another scar, but wounds heal. They make us stronger.

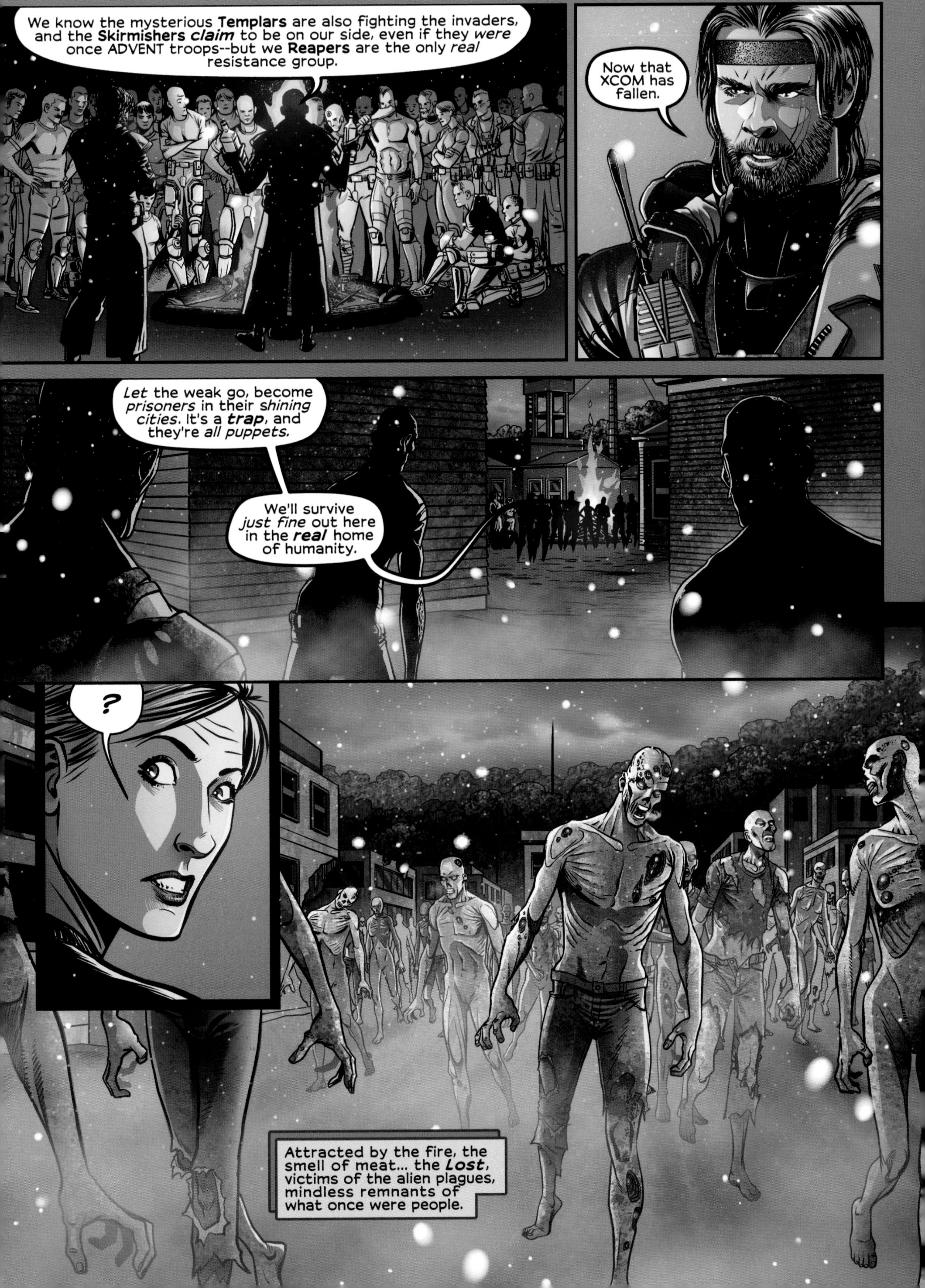
We know the mysterious **Templars** are also fighting the invaders, and the **Skirmishers** ***claim*** to be on our side, even if they *were* once ADVENT troops--but we **Reapers** are the only *real* resistance group.
Now that XCOM has fallen.
Let the weak go, become *prisoners* in their *shining cities*. It's a ***trap***, and they're *all puppets*.
We'll survive *just fine* out here in the ***real*** home of humanity.
?
Attracted by the fire, the smell of meat... the ***Lost***, victims of the alien plagues, mindless remnants of what once were people.

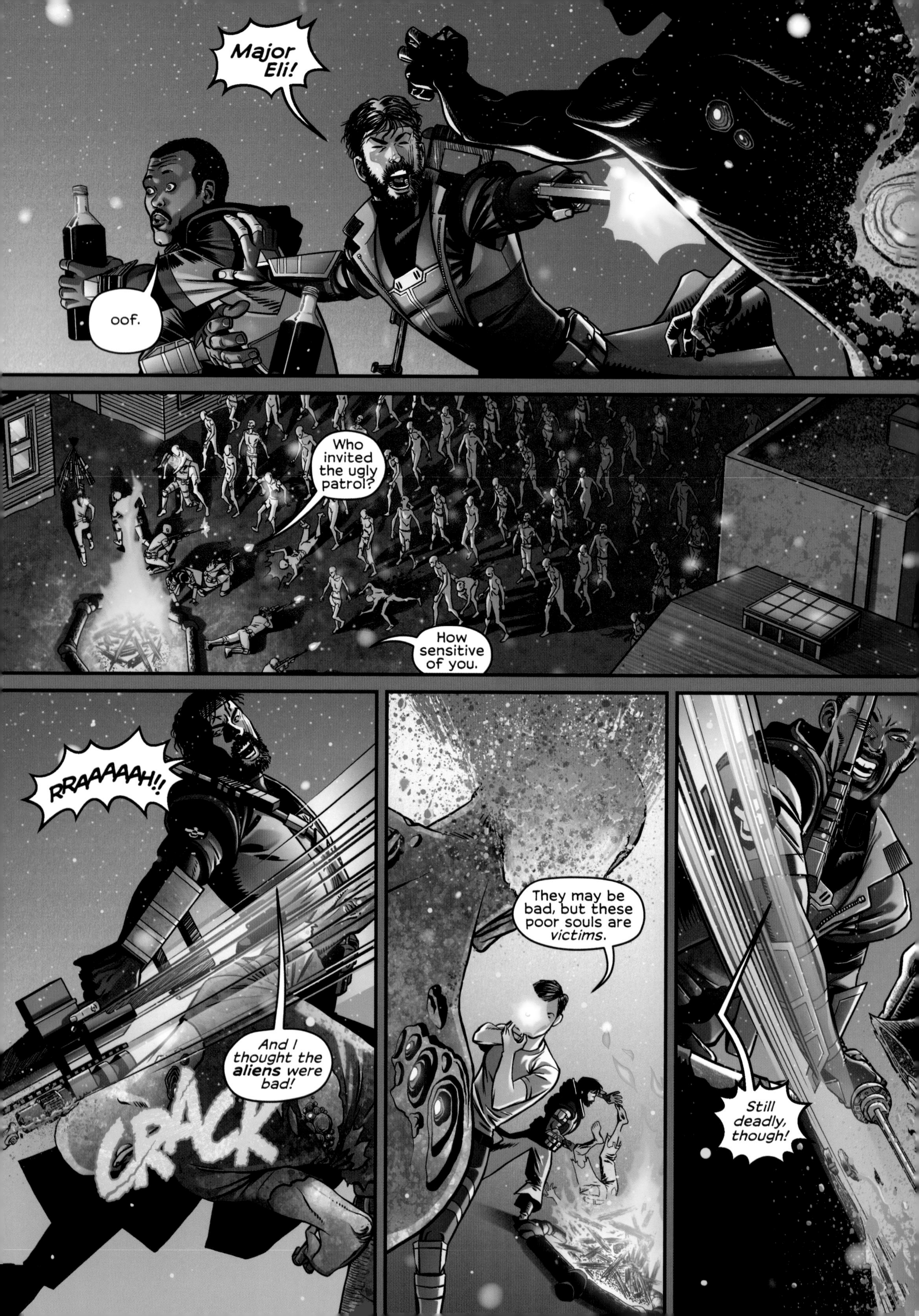
Major Eli!
oof.
Who invited the ugly patrol?
How sensitive of you.
RRAAAAAH!!
And I thought the **aliens** were bad!
CRACK
They may be bad, but these poor souls are *victims*.
Still deadly, though!

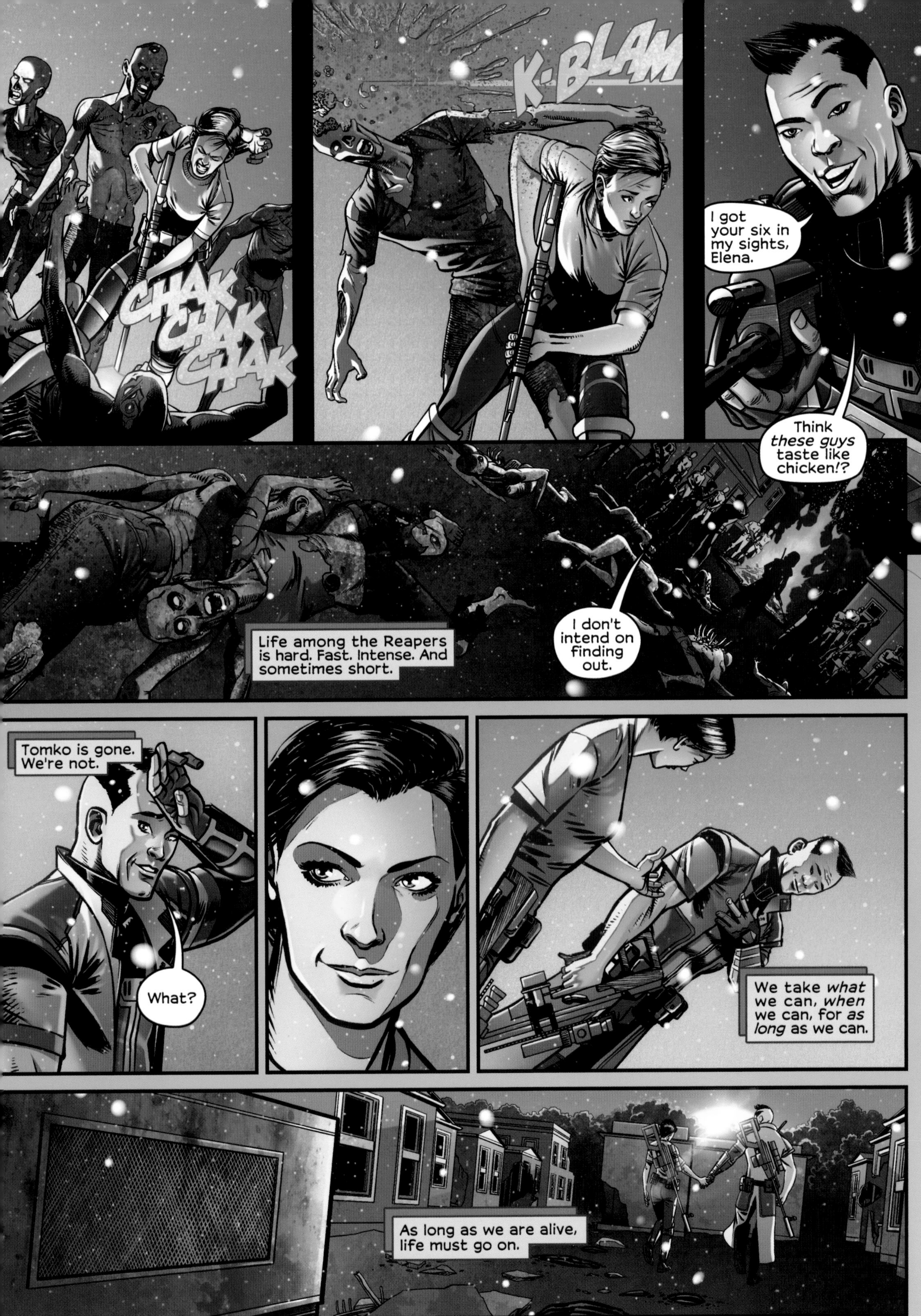
CHAK CHAK CHAK
K-BLAM
I got your six in my sights, Elena.
Think *these guys* taste like chicken!?
Life among the Reapers is hard. Fast. Intense. And sometimes short.
I don't intend on finding out.
Tomko is gone. We're not.
What?
We take *what* we can, *when* we can, for *as long* as we can.
As long as we are alive, life must go on.

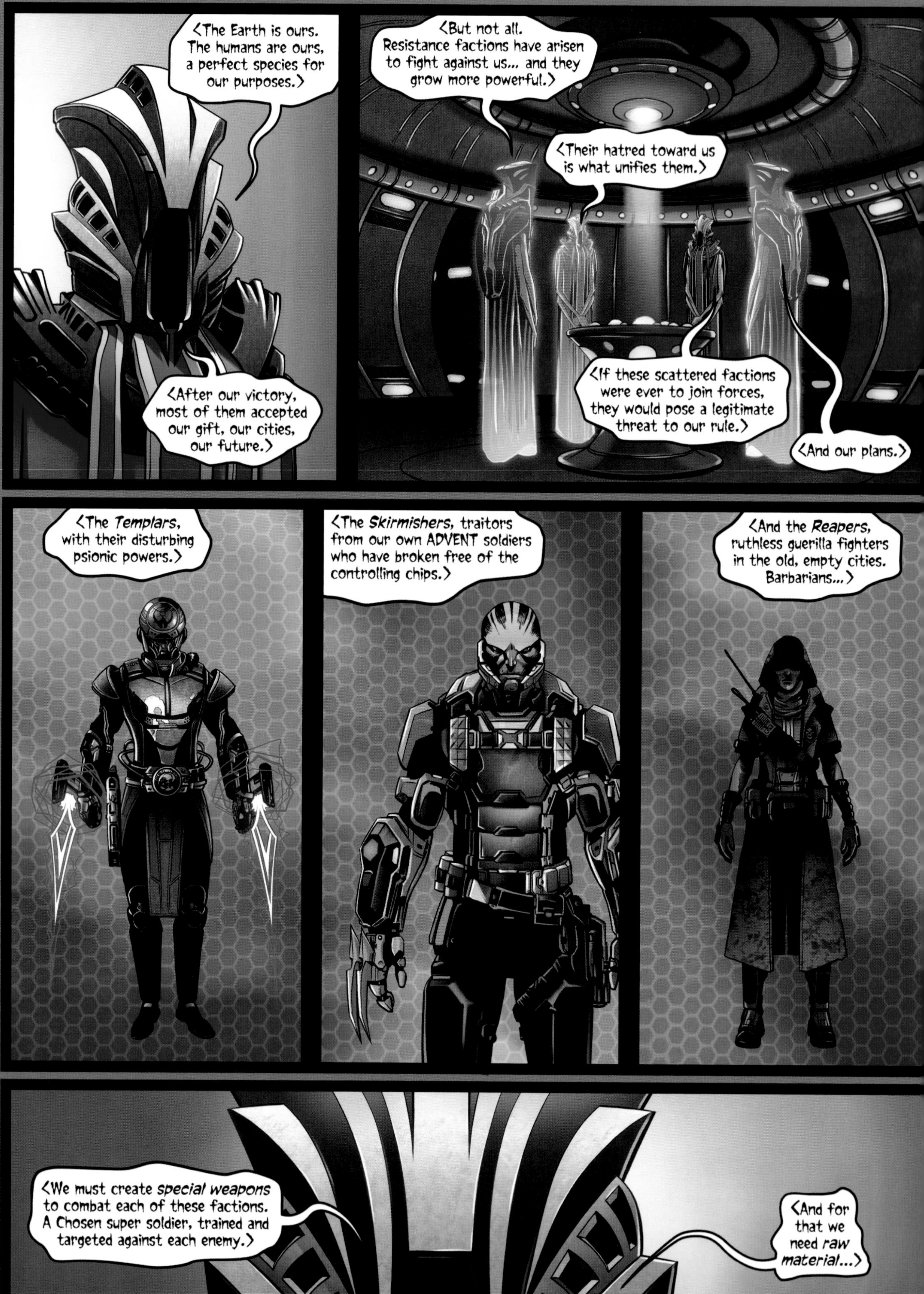
<The Earth is ours. The humans are ours, a perfect species for our purposes.>
<After our victory, most of them accepted our gift, our cities, our future.>
<But not all. Resistance factions have arisen to fight against us... and they grow more powerful.>
<Their hatred toward us is what unifies them.>
<If these scattered factions were ever to join forces, they would pose a legitimate threat to our rule.>
<And our plans.>
<The *Templars*, with their disturbing psionic powers.>
<The *Skirmishers*, traitors from our own ADVENT soldiers who have broken free of the controlling chips.>
<And the *Reapers*, ruthless guerilla fighters in the old, empty cities. Barbarians...>
<We must create *special weapons* to combat each of these factions. A Chosen super soldier, trained and targeted against each enemy.>
<And for that we need *raw material*...>

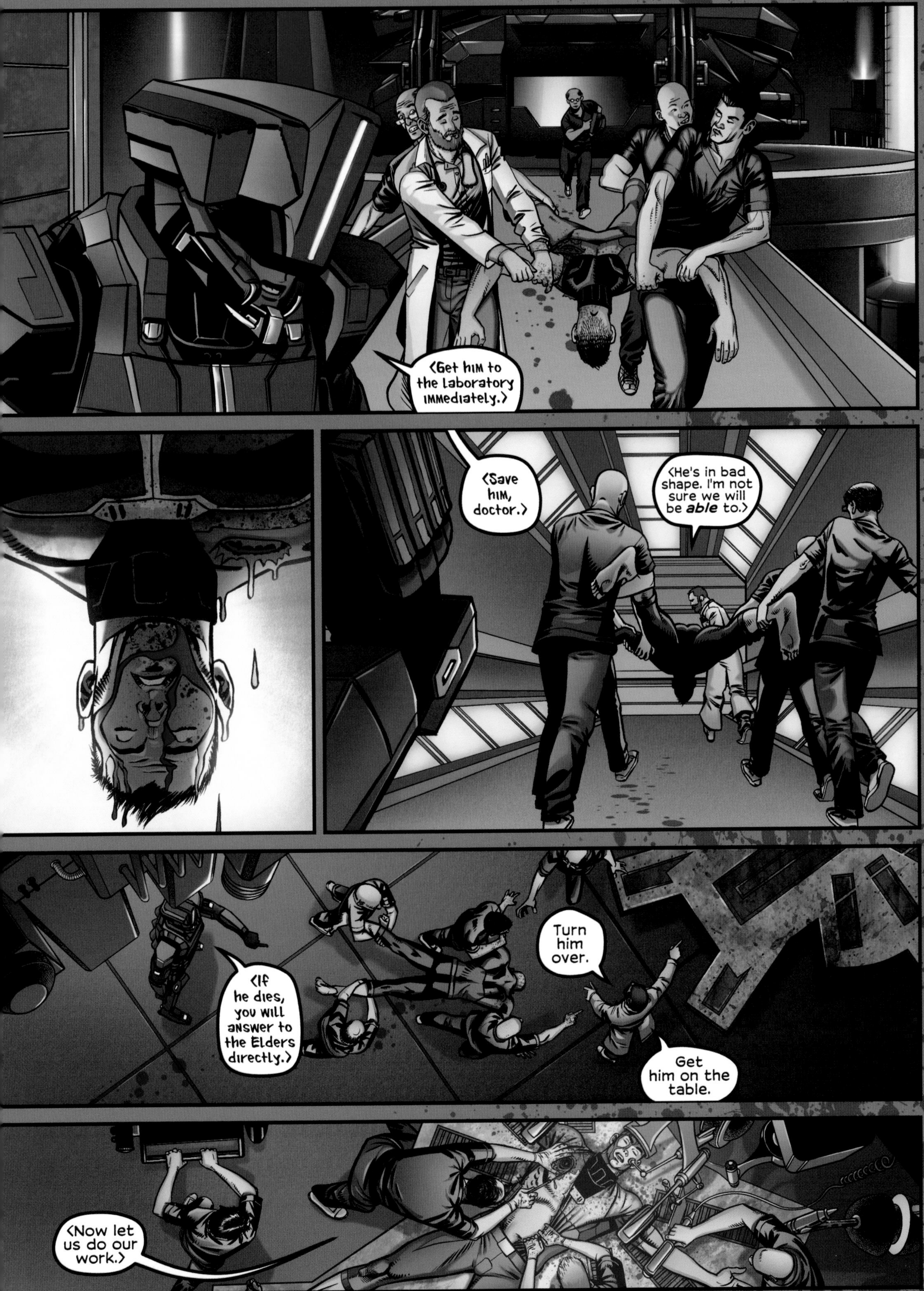
<Get him to the laboratory immediately.>
<Save him, doctor.>
<He's in bad shape. I'm not sure we will be *able* to.>
<If he dies, you will answer to the Elders directly.>
Turn him over.
Get him on the table.
<Now let us do our work.>

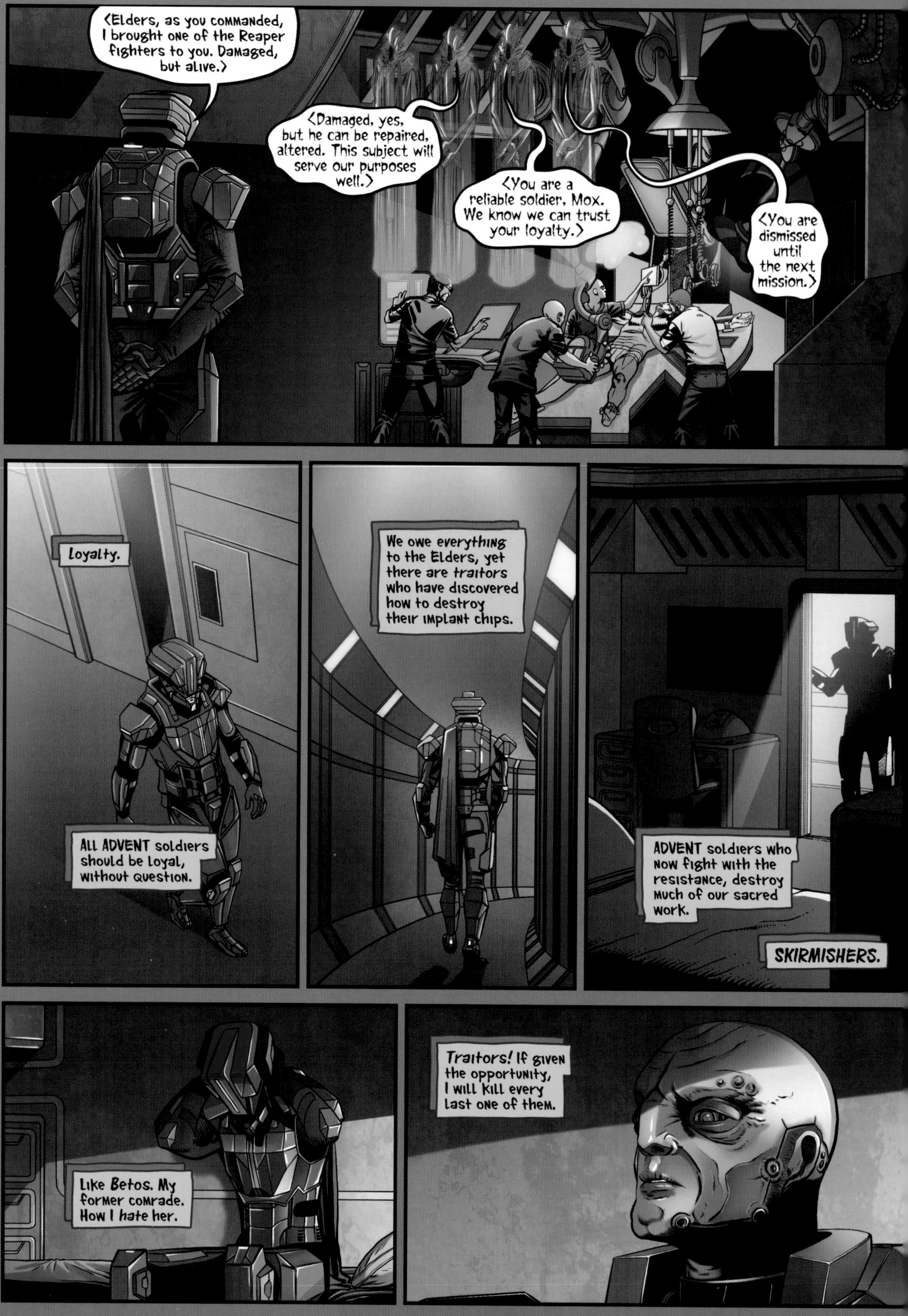
<Elders, as you commanded, I brought one of the Reaper fighters to you. Damaged, but alive.>
<Damaged, yes, but he can be repaired, altered. This subject will serve our purposes well.>
<You are a reliable soldier, Mox. We know we can trust your loyalty.>
<You are dismissed until the next mission.>
Loyalty.
All ADVENT soldiers should be loyal, without question.
We owe everything to the Elders, yet there are traitors who have discovered how to destroy their implant chips.
ADVENT soldiers who now fight with the resistance, destroy much of our sacred work.
SKIRMISHERS.
Like Betos. My former comrade. How I hate her.
Traitors! If given the opportunity, I will kill every last one of them.

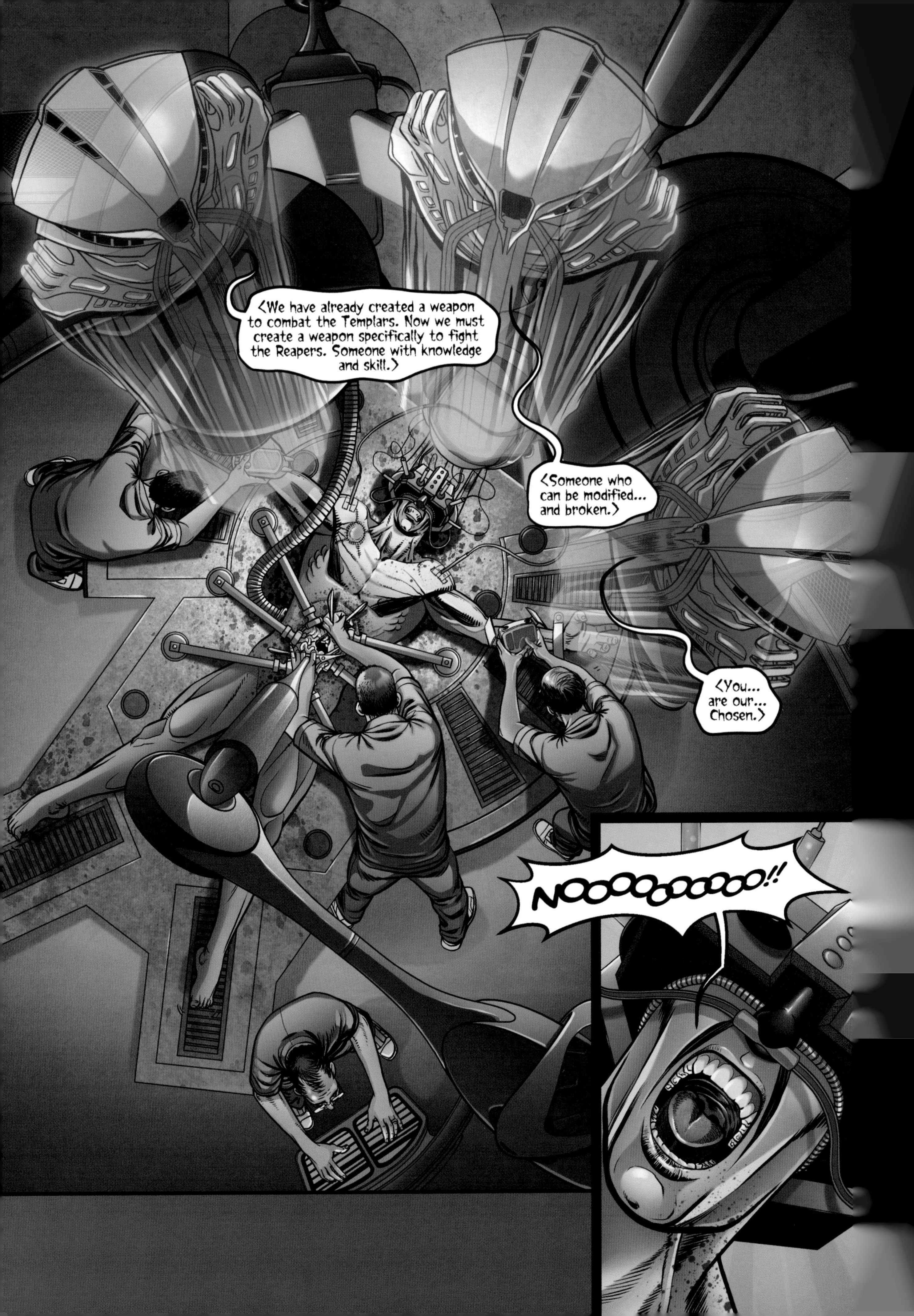

<We have already created a weapon to combat the Templars. Now we must create a weapon specifically to fight the Reapers. Someone with knowledge and skill.>
<Someone who can be modified... and broken.>
<You... are our... Chosen.>
NOOOOOOOOOO!!

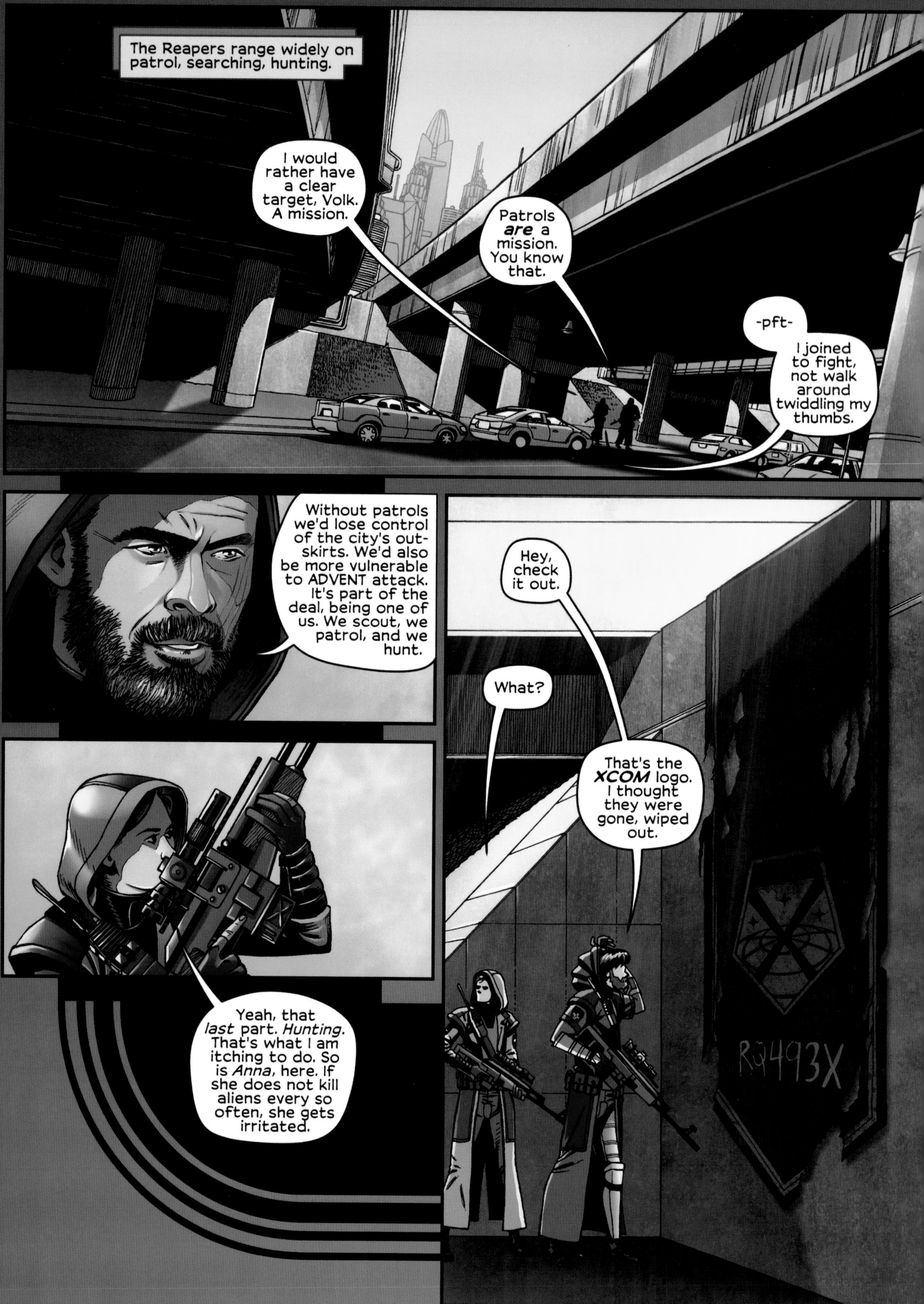

The Reapers range widely on patrol, searching, hunting.
I would rather have a clear target, Volk. A mission.
Patrols *are* a mission. You know that.
-pft-
I joined to fight, not walk around twiddling my thumbs.
Without patrols we'd lose control of the city's out-skirts. We'd also be more vulnerable to ADVENT attack. It's part of the deal, being one of us. We scout, we patrol, and we hunt.
Yeah, that *last* part. *Hunting*. That's what I am itching to do. So is *Anna*, here. If she does not kill aliens every so often, she gets irritated.
Hey, check it out.
What?
That's the ***XCOM*** logo. I thought they were gone, wiped out.
RQ493X

I was always part of my own group of fighters up in Alaska. But XCOM? They were organized. They had their s#!+ together.

We really thought they were humanity's best hope.

"XCOM was led by a brilliant *commander* who vowed never to surrender."

"I never actually joined XCOM--there were many resistance groups--but I fought alongside *Central Officer Bradford* when our missions aligned."

"We put up a hell of a fight; we weren't going to just *hand* the Earth to them."

"But when the *Commander* was... Captured? Killed?

XCOM fell apart. Earth's governments surrendered to the invaders not long after that."

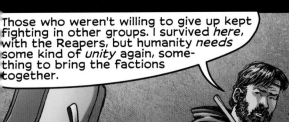

Those who weren't willing to give up kept fighting in other groups. I survived *here*, with the Reapers, but humanity *needs* some kind of *unity* again, something to bring the factions together.

And *this*?

This is a *frequency code*.

And it's *fresh*.

RQ493X

25

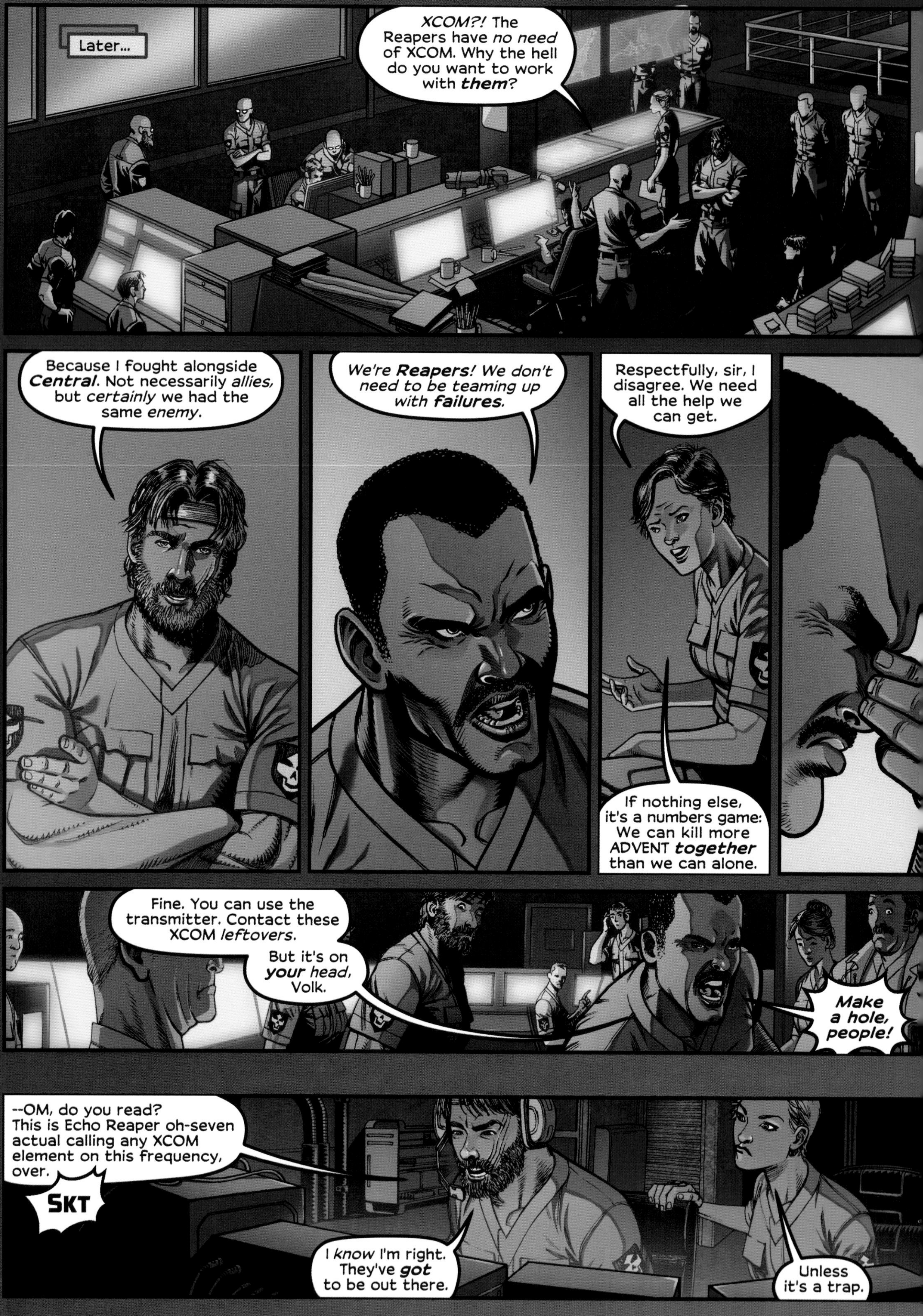
Later...
XCOM?! The Reapers have no need of XCOM. Why the hell do you want to work with them?
Because I fought alongside Central. Not necessarily allies, but certainly we had the same enemy.
We're Reapers! We don't need to be teaming up with failures.
Respectfully, sir, I disagree. We need all the help we can get.
If nothing else, it's a numbers game: We can kill more ADVENT together than we can alone.
Fine. You can use the transmitter. Contact these XCOM leftovers.
But it's on your head, Volk.
Make a hole, people!
--OM, do you read? This is Echo Reaper oh-seven actual calling any XCOM element on this frequency, over.
SKT
I know I'm right. They've got to be out there.
Unless it's a trap.

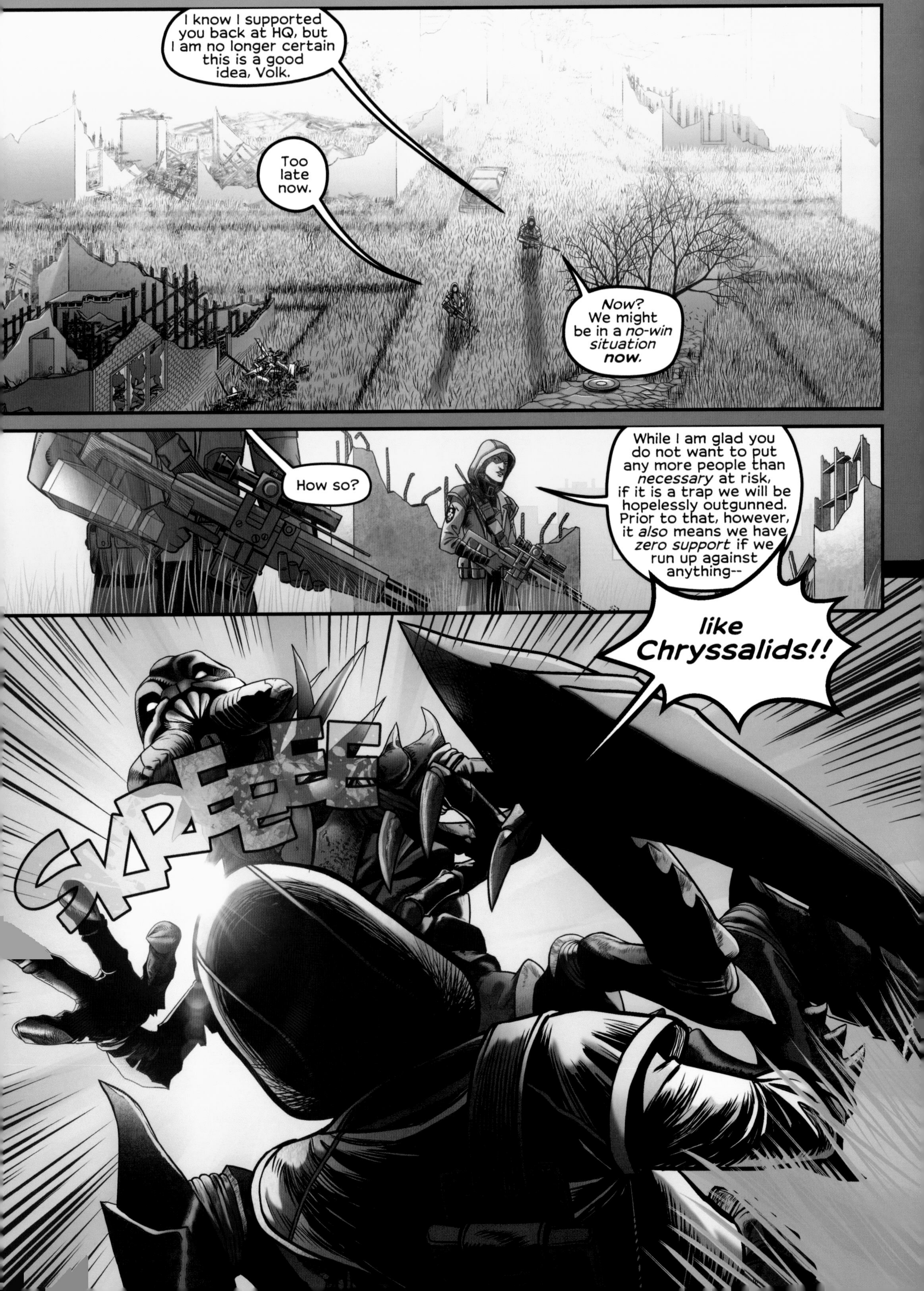
I know I supported you back at HQ, but I am no longer certain this is a good idea, Volk.
Too late now.
Now? We might be in a *no-win situation* **now.**
How so?
While I am glad you do not want to put any more people than *necessary* at risk, if it is a trap we will be hopelessly outgunned. Prior to that, however, it *also* means we have *zero support* if we run up against anything--
like Chryssalids!!

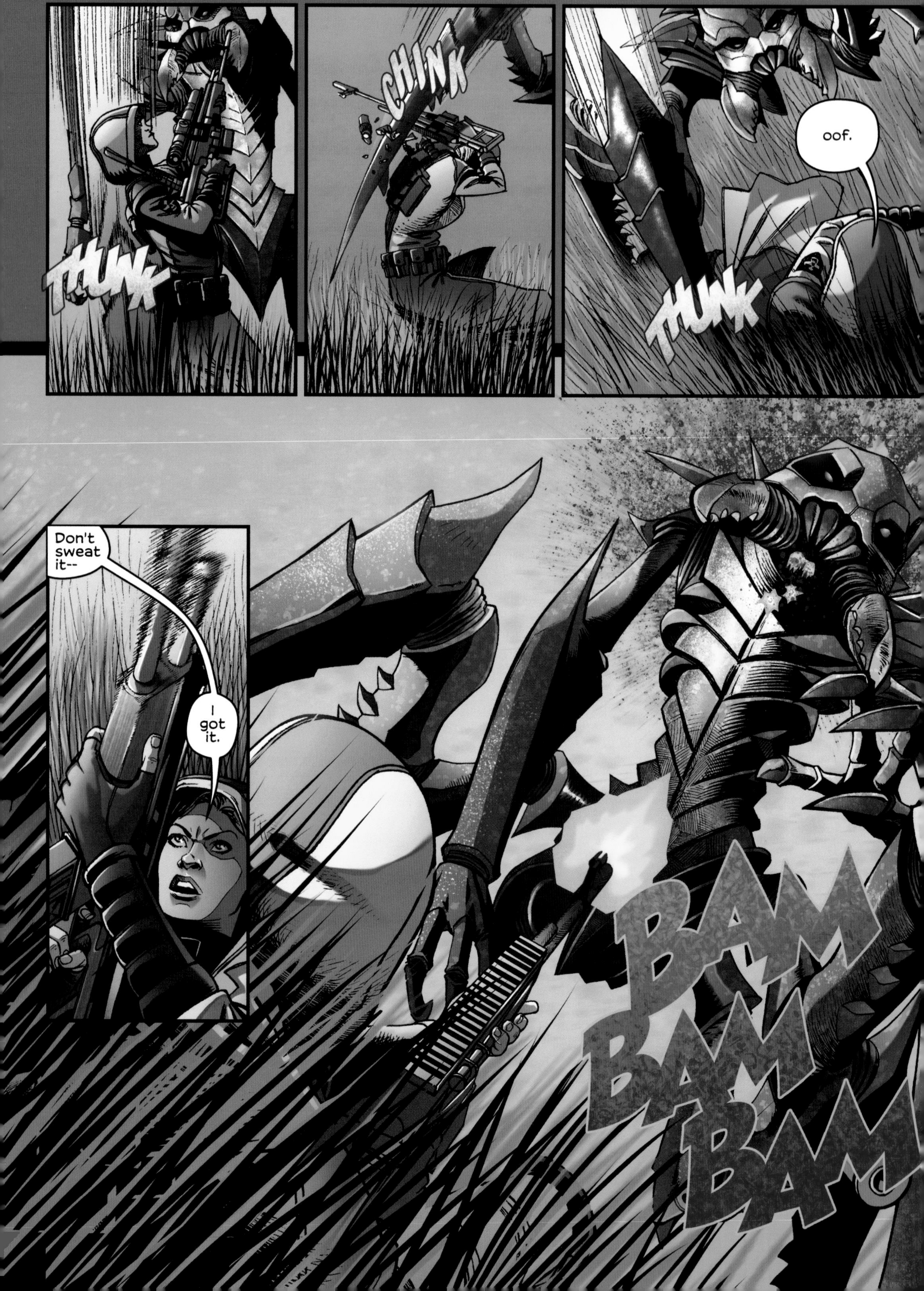
THUNK
CHINK
oof.
THUNK
Don't sweat it--
I got it.
BAM
BAM
BAM

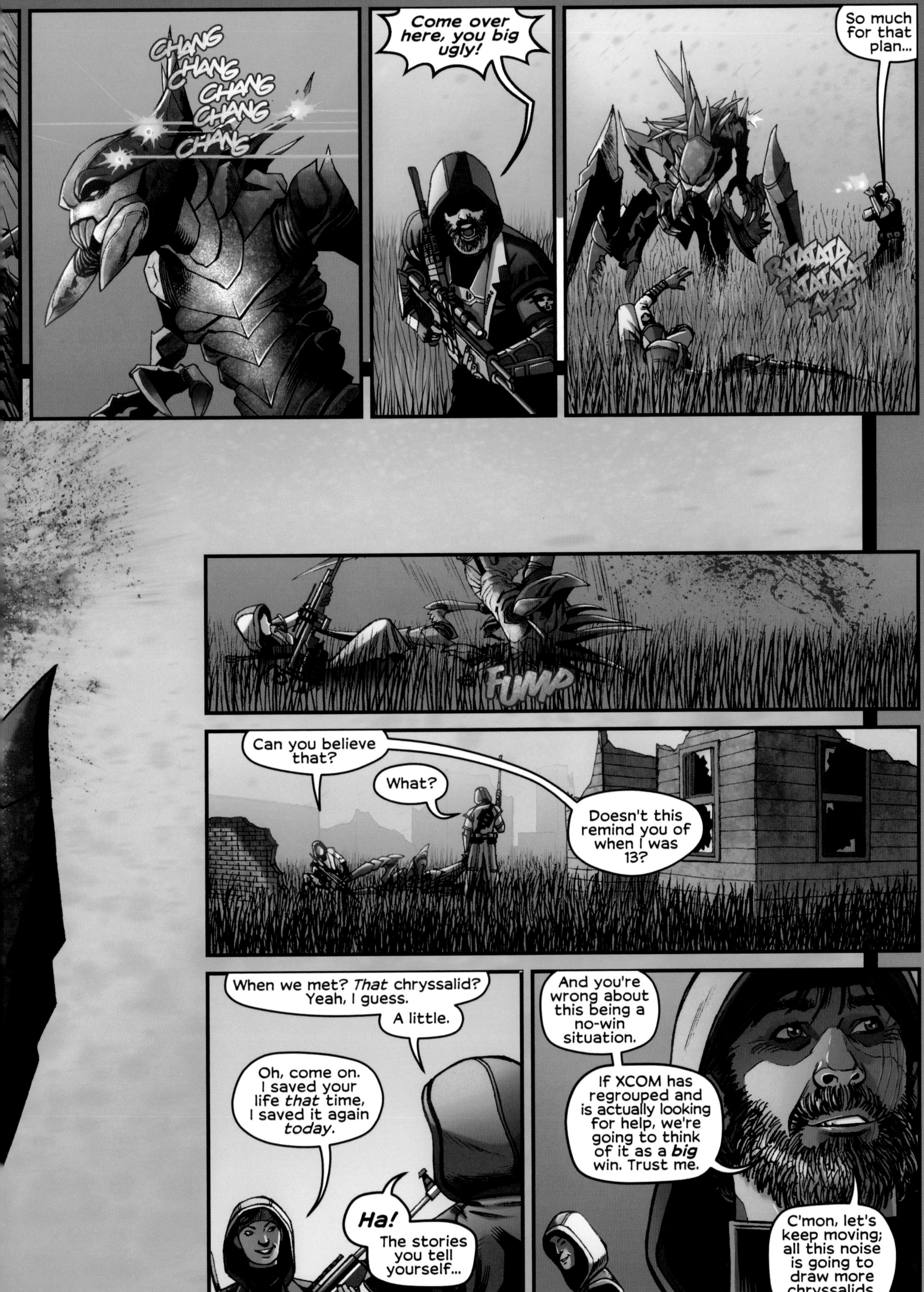

CHANG CHANG CHANG CHANG CHANG
Come over here, you big ugly!
So much for that plan...
RATATATATATATATATATAT
FUMP
Can you believe that?
What?
Doesn't this remind you of when I was 13?
When we met? *That* chryssalid? Yeah, I guess.
A little.
Oh, come on. I saved your life *that* time, I saved it again *today*.
Ha!
The stories you tell yourself...
And you're wrong about this being a no-win situation.
If XCOM has regrouped and is actually looking for help, we're going to think of it as a ***big*** win. Trust me.
C'mon, let's keep moving; all this noise is going to draw more chryssalids.

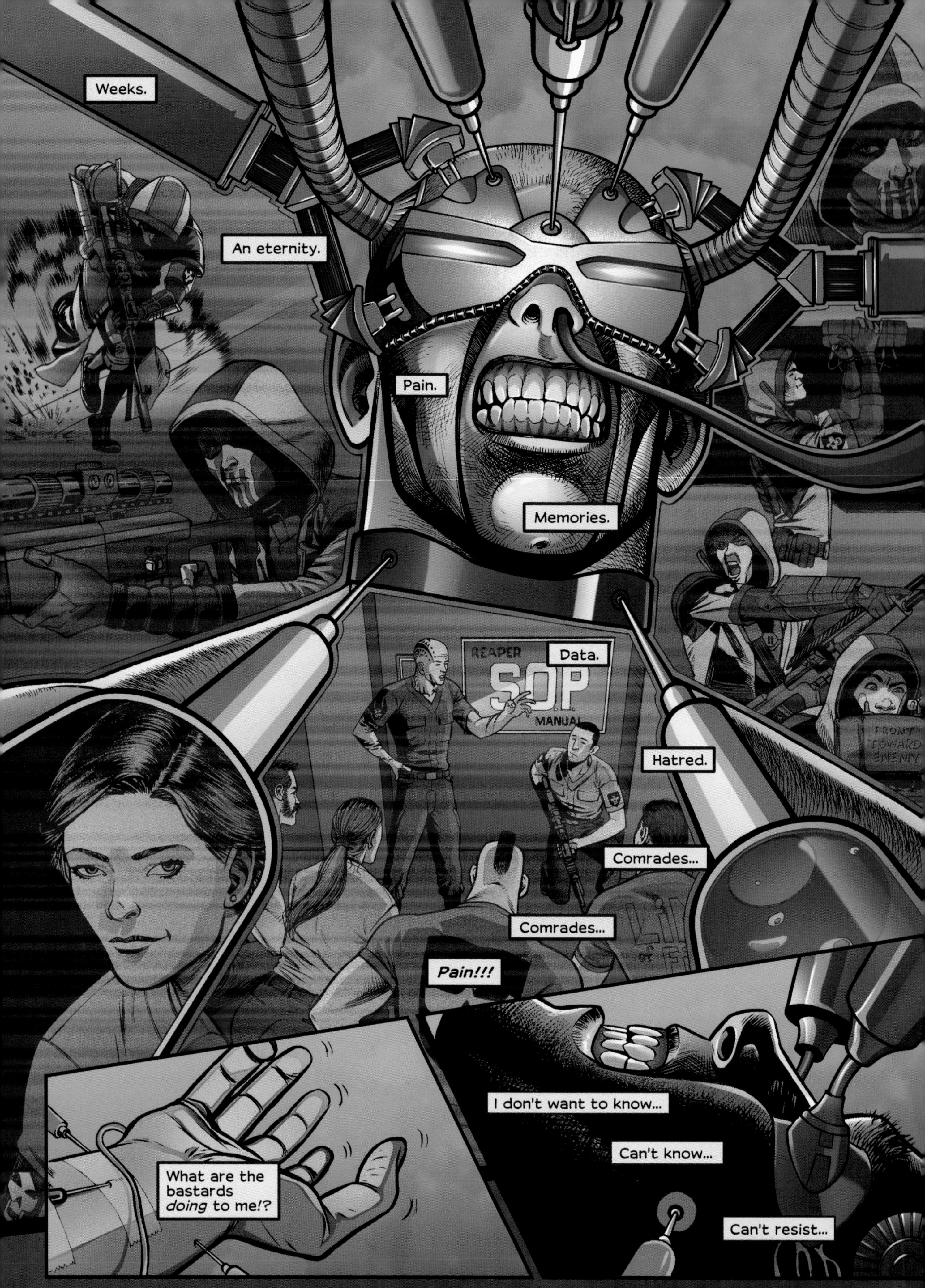
Weeks.
An eternity.
Pain.
Memories.
REAPER
S.O.P.
MANUAL
Data.
Hatred.
FRONT TOWARD ENEMY
Comrades...
Comrades...
Pain!!!
I don't want to know...
Can't know...
What are the bastards *doing* to me!?
Can't resist...

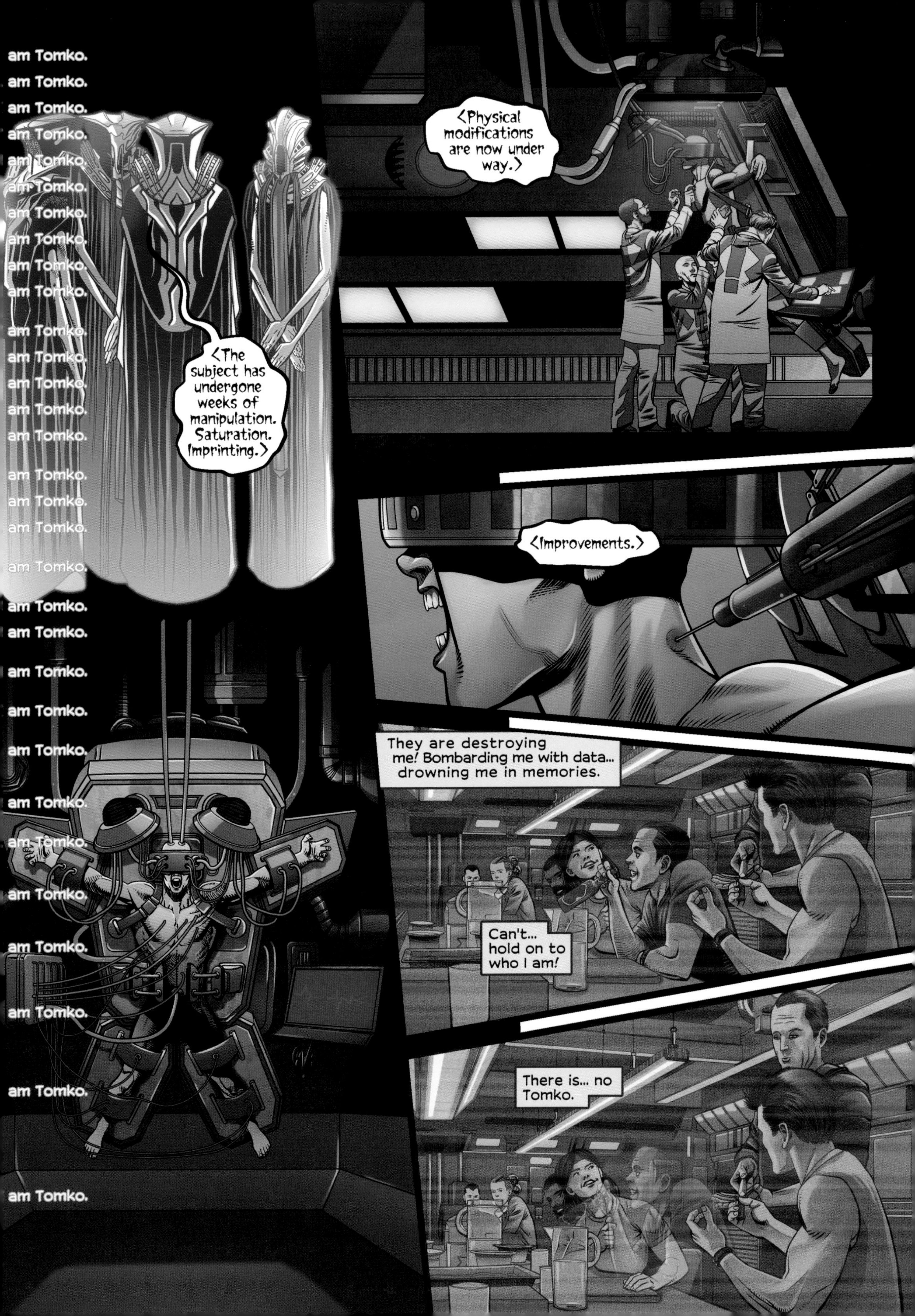
am Tomko.
am Tomko.
am Tomko.
am Tomko.
am Tomko.
am Tomko.
am Tomko.
am Tomko.
am Tomko.
am Tomko.
am Tomko.
am Tomko.
am Tomko.
am Tomko.
am Tomko.
am Tomko.
am Tomko.
am Tomko.
am Tomko.
am Tomko.
am Tomko.
am Tomko.
am Tomko.
am Tomko.
am Tomko.
am Tomko.
am Tomko.
am Tomko.
am Tomko.
am Tomko.
am Tomko.
<The subject has undergone weeks of manipulation. Saturation. Imprinting.>
<Physical modifications are now under way.>
<Improvements.>
They are destroying me! Bombarding me with data... drowning me in memories.
Can't... hold on to who I am!
There is... no Tomko.

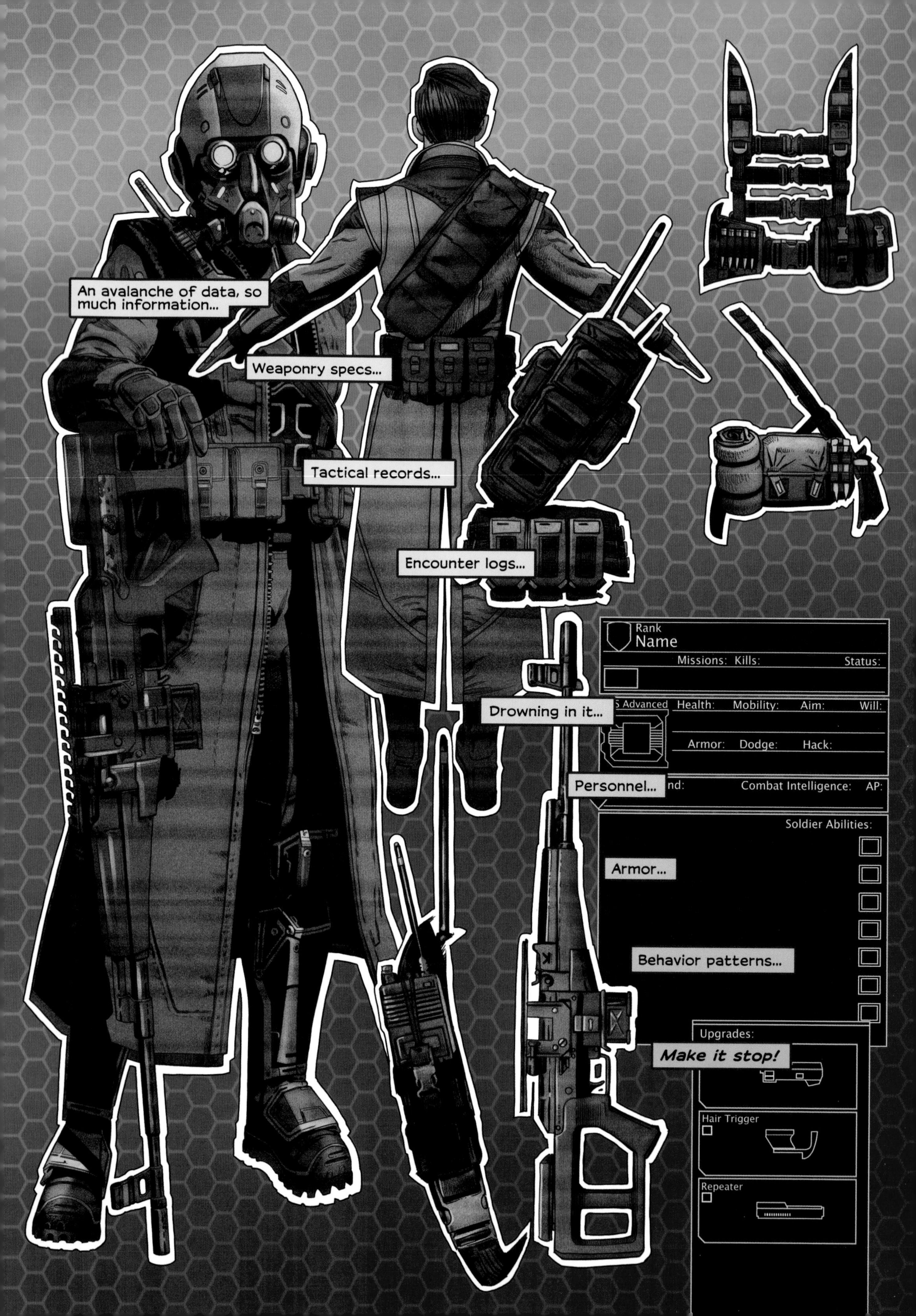

An avalanche of data, so much information...
Weaponry specs...
Tactical records...
Encounter logs...
Rank
Name
Missions: Kills: Status:
S Advanced Health: Mobility: Aim: Will:
Armor: Dodge: Hack:
Drowning in it...
Personnel...
nd: Combat Intelligence: AP:
Soldier Abilities:
Armor...
Behavior patterns...
Upgrades:
Make it stop!
Hair Trigger
Repeater

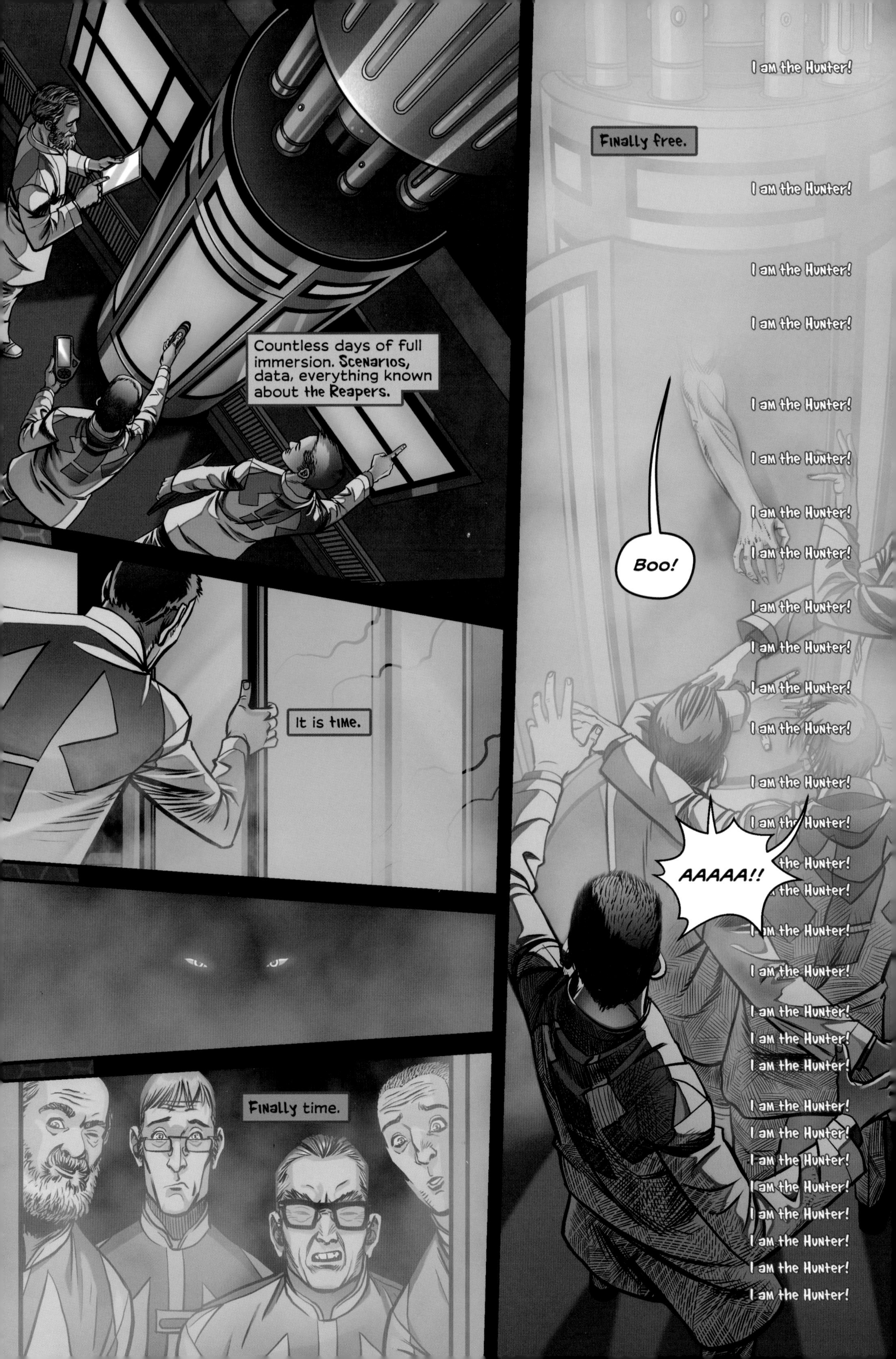
Countless days of full immersion. Scenarios, data, everything known about the Reapers.
It is time.
Finally time.
I am the Hunter!
Finally free.
I am the Hunter!
I am the Hunter!
I am the Hunter!
I am the Hunter!
I am the Hunter!
I am the Hunter!
Boo!
I am the Hunter!
I am the Hunter!
I am the Hunter!
I am the Hunter!
I am the Hunter!
I am the Hunter!
I am the Hunter!
AAAAA!!
the Hunter!
the Hunter!
am the Hunter!
I am the Hunter!
I am the Hunter!
I am the Hunter!
I am the Hunter!
I am the Hunter!
I am the Hunter!
I am the Hunter!
I am the Hunter!
I am the Hunter!
I am the Hunter!
I am the Hunter!
I am the Hunter!

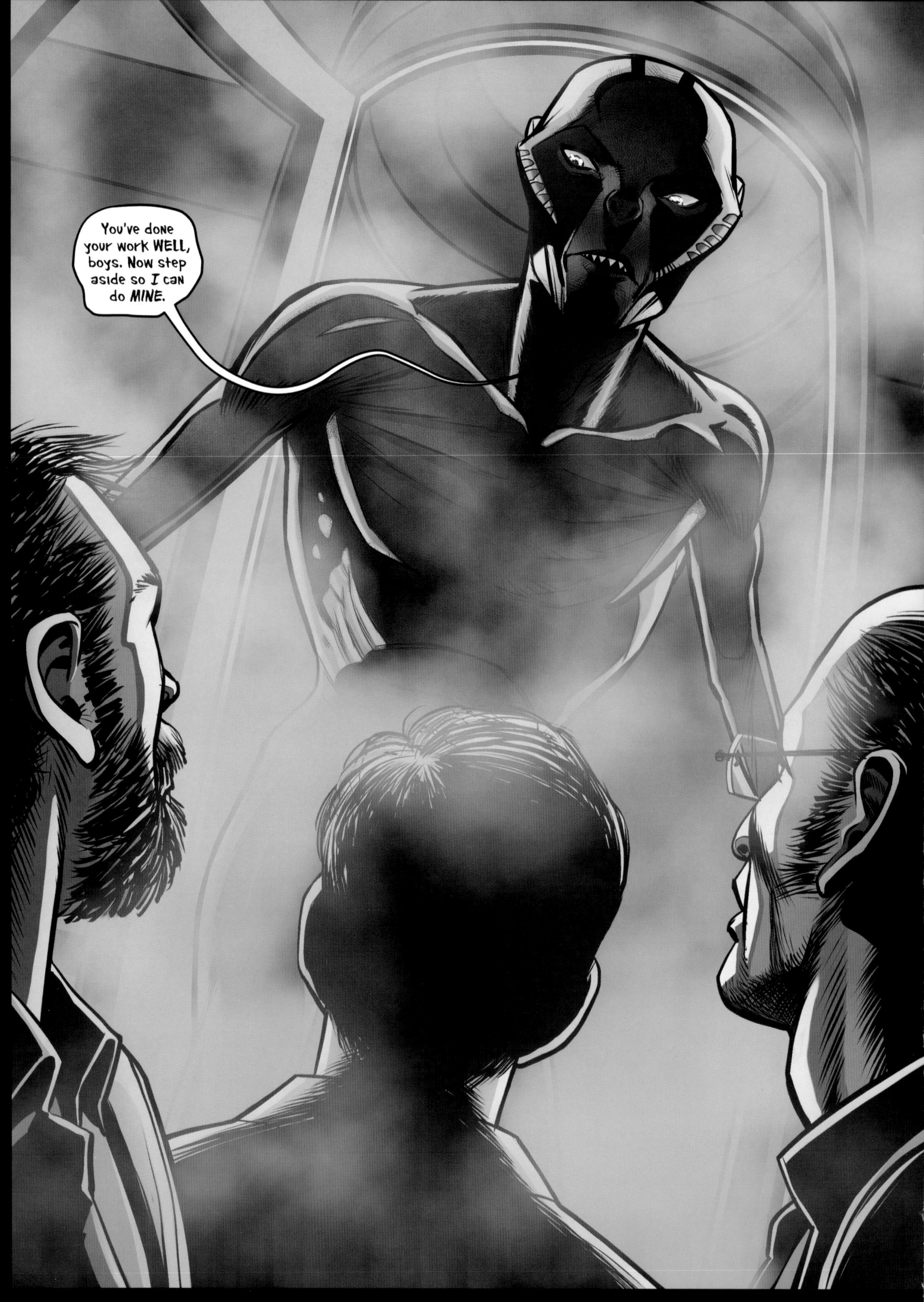
You've done your work WELL, boys. Now step aside so I can do MINE.

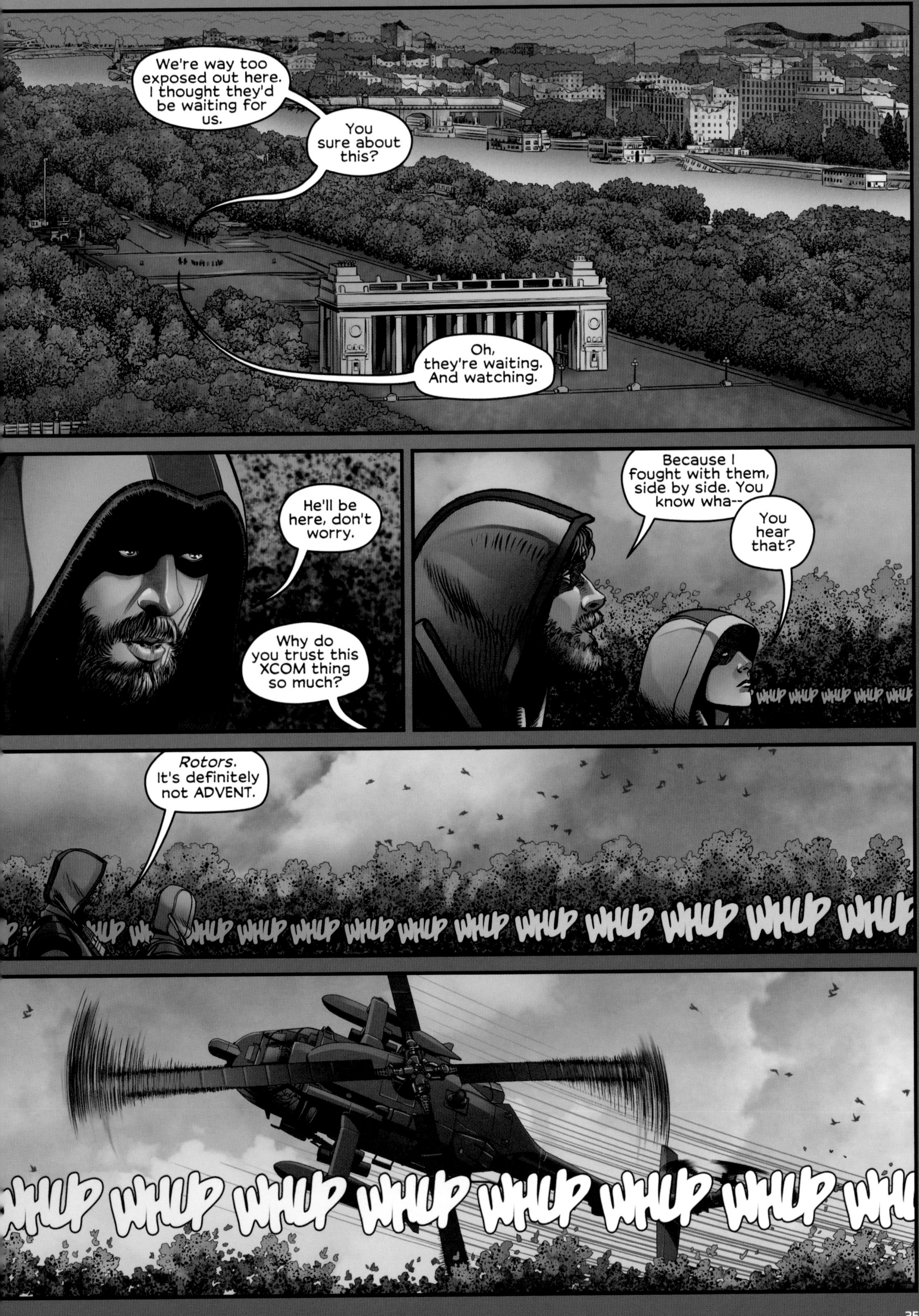
We're way too exposed out here. I thought they'd be waiting for us.
You sure about this?
Oh, they're waiting. And watching.
He'll be here, don't worry.
Why do you trust this XCOM thing so much?
Because I fought with them, side by side. You know wha--
You hear that?
WHUP WHUP WHUP WHUP WHUP
Rotors. It's definitely not ADVENT.
WHUP WHUP WHUP WHUP WHUP WHUP WHUP WHUP WHUP WHUP WHUP
WHUP WHUP WHUP WHUP WHUP WHUP WHUP WHUP

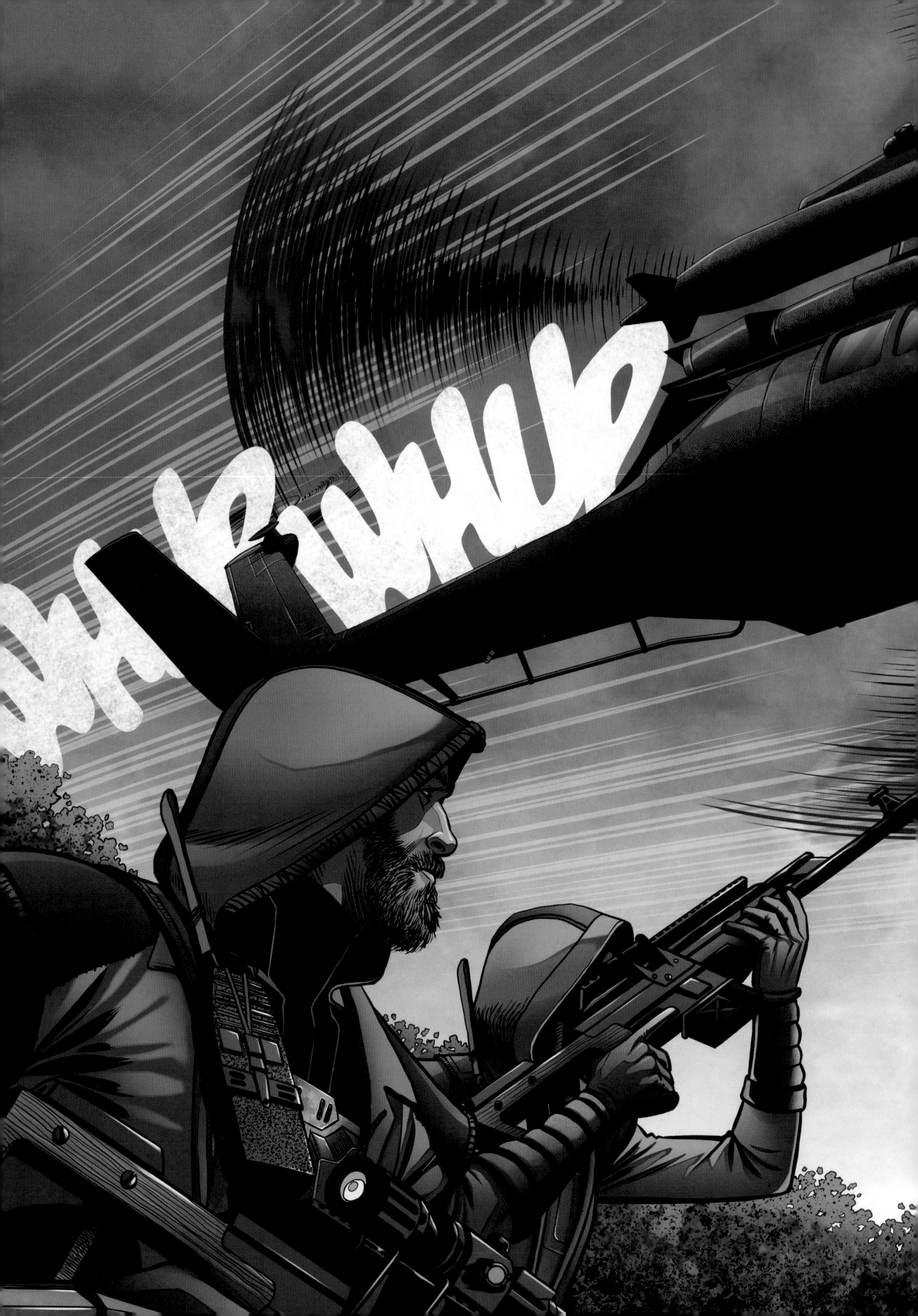

Good to see you again, Bradford!

Elena, this is **Central Officer Bradford.** We don't always see eye to eye, but, well... Like I told you, he recruited me back in my hometown at the beginning of the invasion.

You went your own way, but we **still** fight the same enemy.

Pleased to meet you, Elena. Welcome to **XCOM.**

We're not XCOM.

I didn't think there was much left of XCOM after the surrender... after the **commander** was killed.

Captured--not killed. We're still looking, and I haven't given up hope.

Come with me. I'll show you what we've rebuilt. And why we need you.

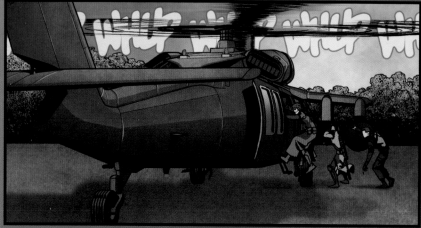

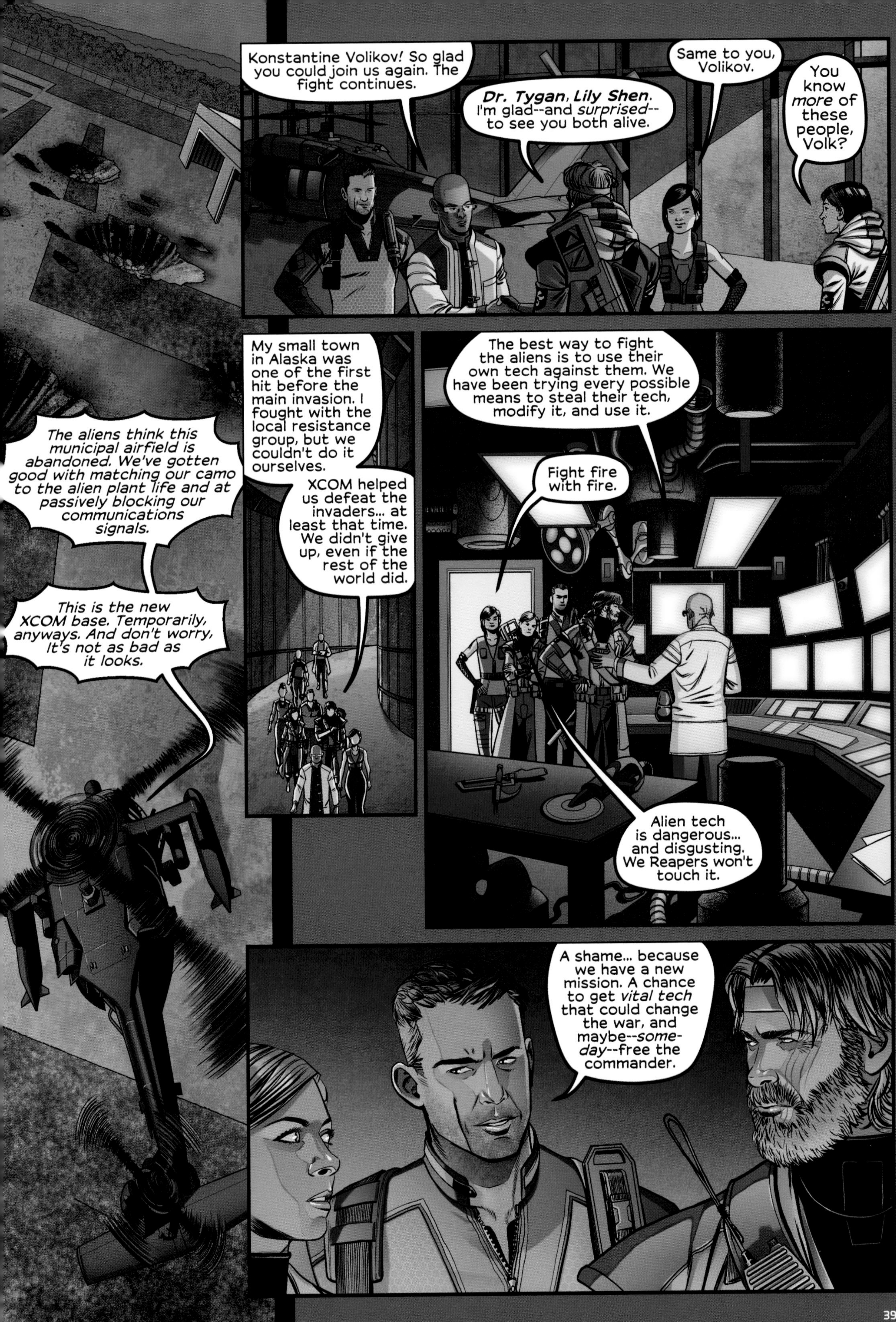
Konstantine Volikov! So glad you could join us again. The fight continues.
Dr. Tygan, Lily Shen. I'm glad--and surprised--to see you both alive.
Same to you, Volikov.
You know more of these people, Volk?
The aliens think this municipal airfield is abandoned. We've gotten good with matching our camo to the alien plant life and at passively blocking our communications signals.
This is the new XCOM base. Temporarily, anyways. And don't worry, It's not as bad as it looks.
My small town in Alaska was one of the first hit before the main invasion. I fought with the local resistance group, but we couldn't do it ourselves.
XCOM helped us defeat the invaders... at least that time. We didn't give up, even if the rest of the world did.
The best way to fight the aliens is to use their own tech against them. We have been trying every possible means to steal their tech, modify it, and use it.
Fight fire with fire.
Alien tech is dangerous... and disgusting. We Reapers won't touch it.
A shame... because we have a new mission. A chance to get vital tech that could change the war, and maybe--someday--free the commander.

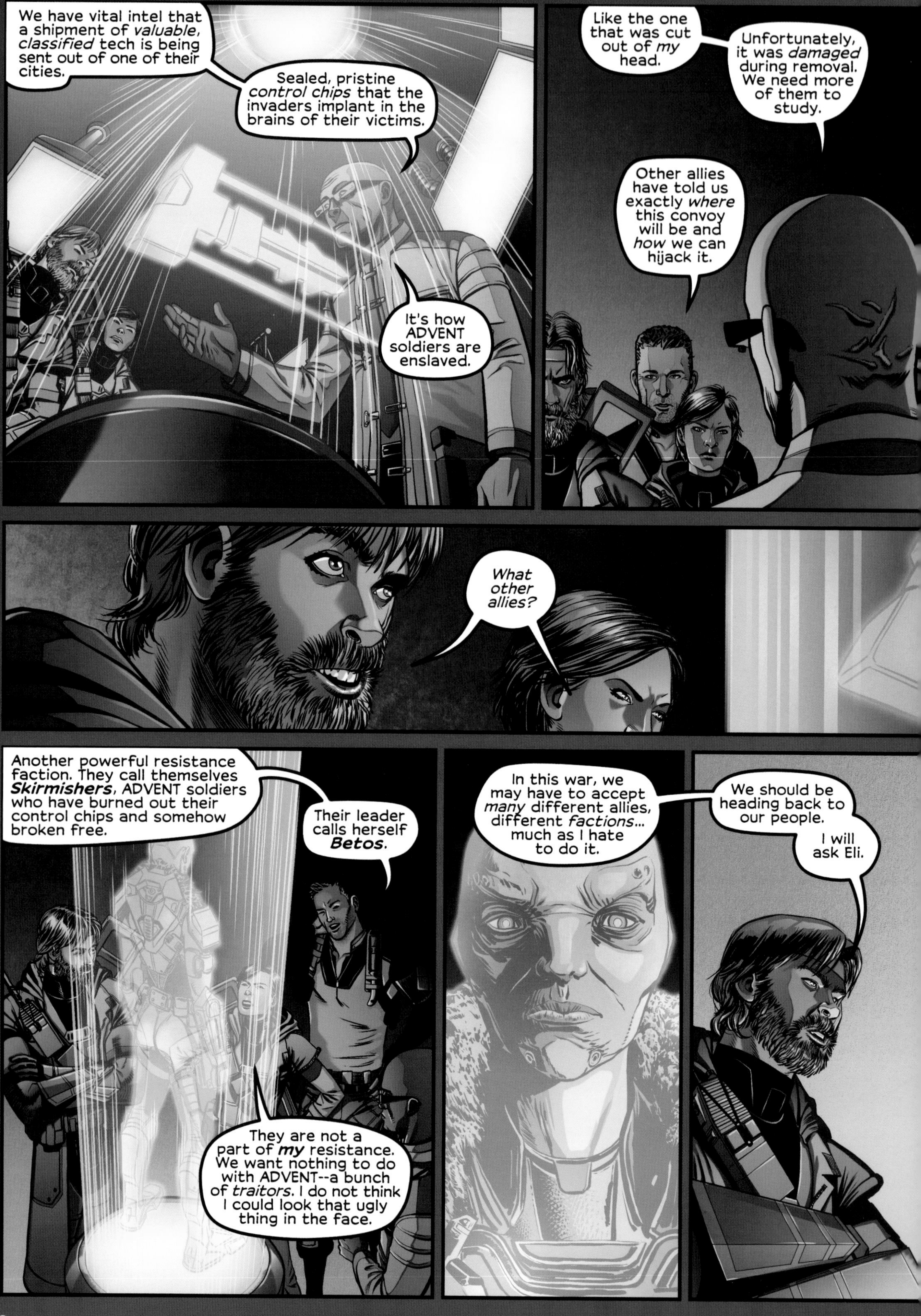
We have vital intel that a shipment of *valuable, classified* tech is being sent out of one of their cities.
Sealed, pristine *control chips* that the invaders implant in the brains of their victims.
It's how ADVENT soldiers are enslaved.
Like the one that was cut out of *my* head.
Unfortunately, it was *damaged* during removal. We need more of them to study.
Other allies have told us exactly *where* this convoy will be and *how* we can hijack it.
What other allies?
Another powerful resistance faction. They call themselves ***Skirmishers***, ADVENT soldiers who have burned out their control chips and somehow broken free.
Their leader calls herself ***Betos***.
They are not a part of ***my*** resistance. We want nothing to do with ADVENT--a bunch of *traitors*. I do not think I could look that ugly thing in the face.
In this war, we may have to accept *many* different allies, different *factions*... much as I hate to do it.
We should be heading back to our people.
I will ask Eli.

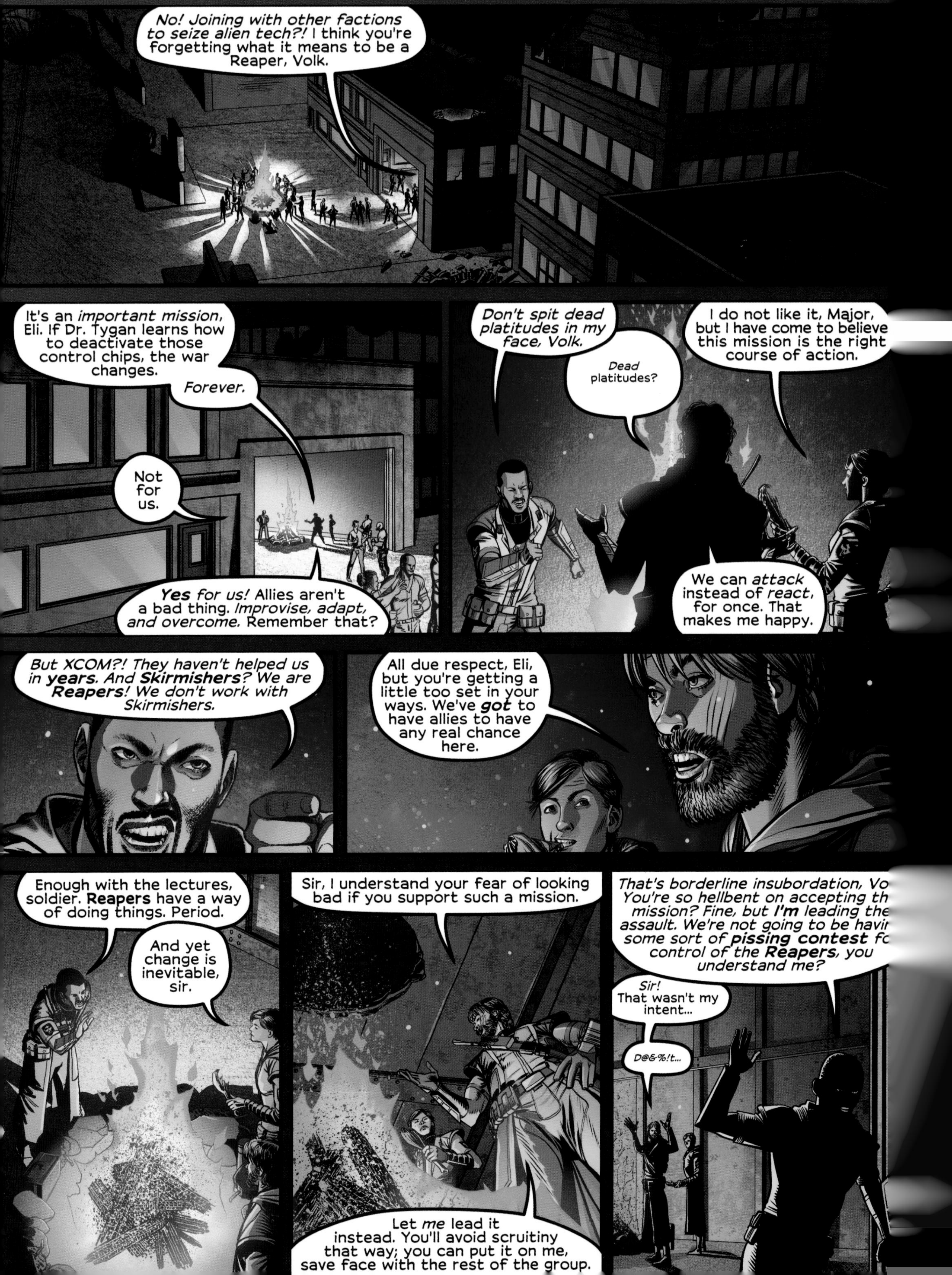
No! Joining with other factions to seize alien tech?! I think you're forgetting what it means to be a Reaper, Volk.
It's an important mission, Eli. If Dr. Tygan learns how to deactivate those control chips, the war changes.
Forever.
Not for us.
Yes for us! Allies aren't a bad thing. Improvise, adapt, and overcome. Remember that?
Don't spit dead platitudes in my face, Volk.
Dead platitudes?
I do not like it, Major, but I have come to believe this mission is the right course of action.
We can attack instead of react, for once. That makes me happy.
But XCOM?! They haven't helped us in years. And Skirmishers? We are Reapers! We don't work with Skirmishers.
All due respect, Eli, but you're getting a little too set in your ways. We've got to have allies to have any real chance here.
Enough with the lectures, soldier. Reapers have a way of doing things. Period.
And yet change is inevitable, sir.
Sir, I understand your fear of looking bad if you support such a mission.
Let me lead it instead. You'll avoid scruitiny that way; you can put it on me, save face with the rest of the group.
That's borderline insubordation, Vo
You're so hellbent on accepting th
mission? Fine, but I'm leading the
assault. We're not going to be havir
some sort of pissing contest fo
control of the Reapers, you understand me?
Sir! That wasn't my intent...
D@&%!t...

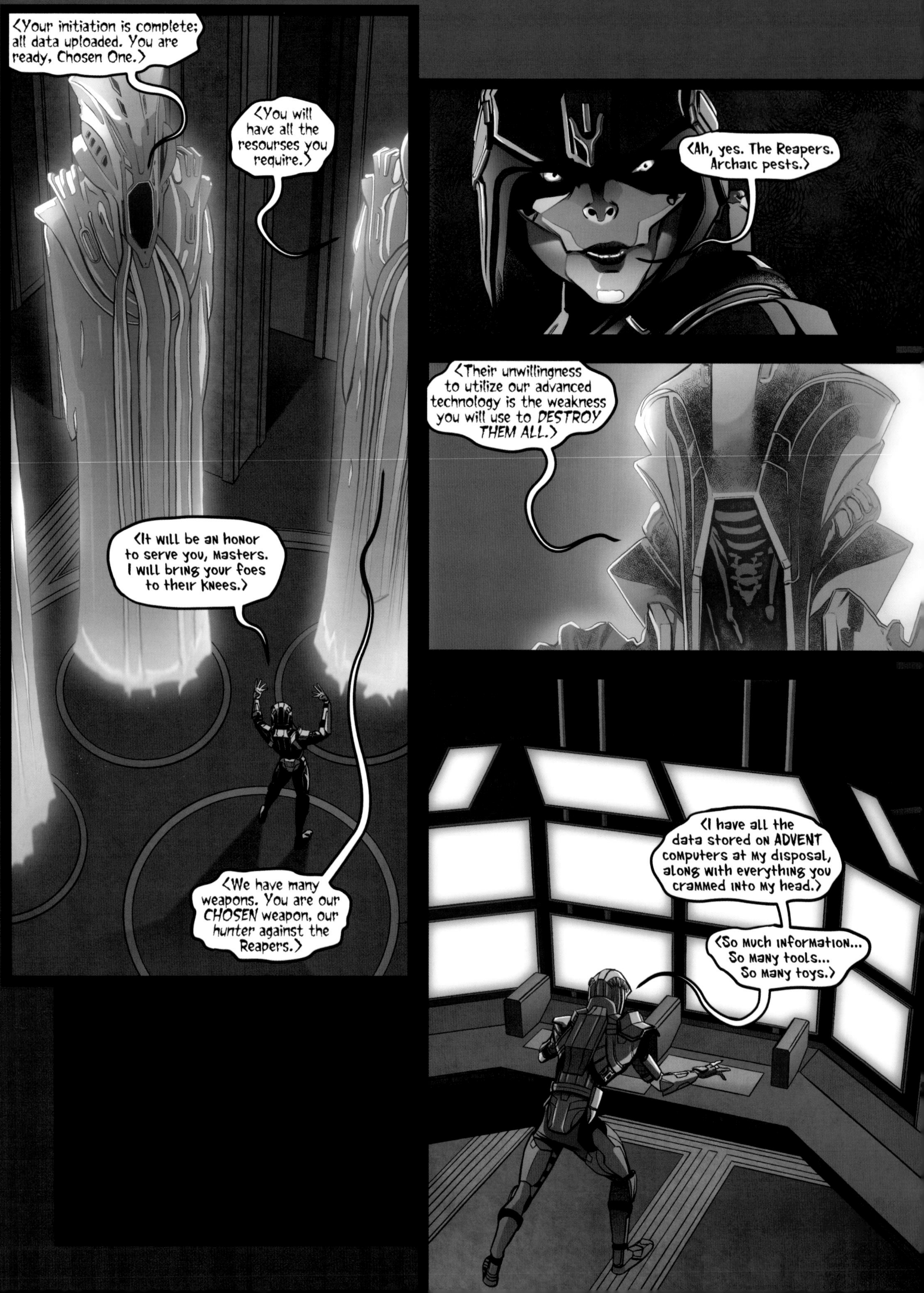

<Your initiation is complete; all data uploaded. You are ready, Chosen One.>
<You will have all the resourses you require.>
<It will be an honor to serve you, Masters. I will bring your foes to their knees.>
<We have many weapons. You are our CHOSEN weapon, our hunter against the Reapers.>
<Ah, yes. The Reapers. Archaic pests.>
<Their unwillingness to utilize our advanced technology is the weakness you will use to DESTROY THEM ALL.>
<I have all the data stored on ADVENT computers at my disposal, along with everything you crammed into my head.>
<So much information... So many tools... So many toys.>

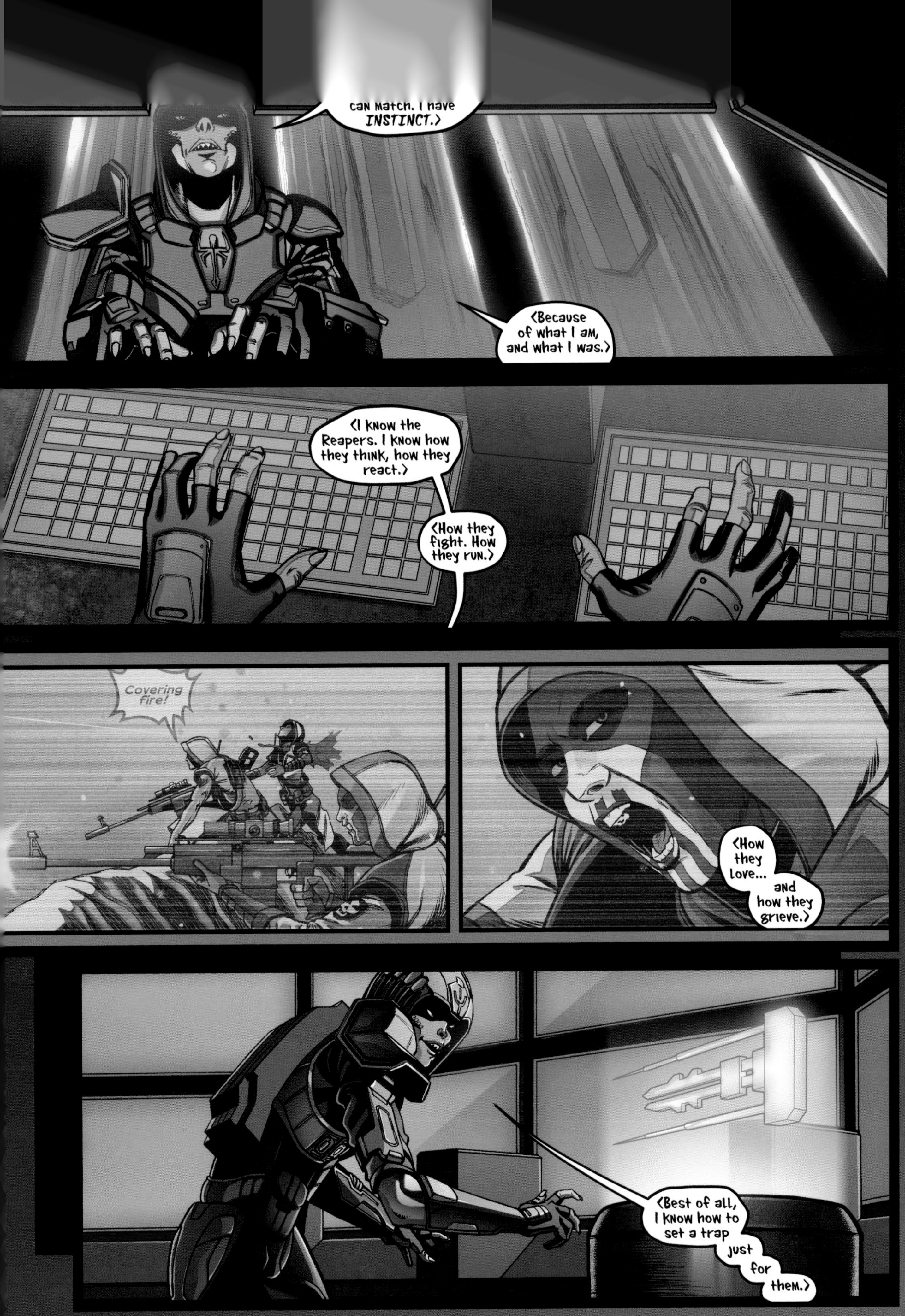
can match. I have INSTINCT.〉
〈Because of what I am, and what I was.〉
〈I know the Reapers. I know how they think, how they react.〉
〈How they fight. How they run.〉
Covering fire!
〈How they love... and how they grieve.〉
〈Best of all, I know how to set a trap just for them.〉

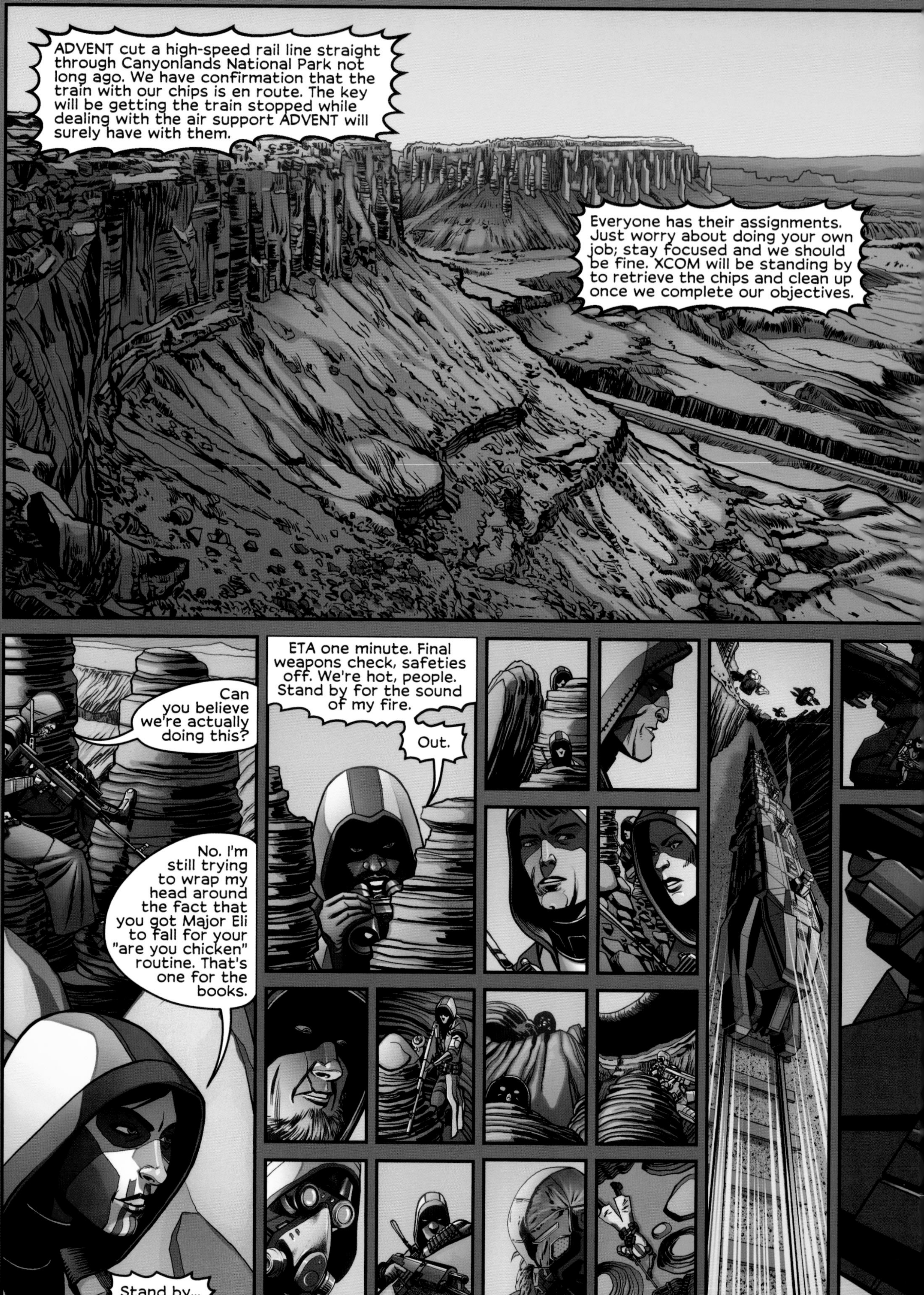

ADVENT cut a high-speed rail line straight through Canyonlands National Park not long ago. We have confirmation that the train with our chips is en route. The key will be getting the train stopped while dealing with the air support ADVENT will surely have with them.
Everyone has their assignments. Just worry about doing your own job; stay focused and we should be fine. XCOM will be standing by to retrieve the chips and clean up once we complete our objectives.
Can you believe we're actually doing this?
No. I'm still trying to wrap my head around the fact that you got Major Eli to fall for your "are you chicken" routine. That's one for the books.
Stand by...
ETA one minute. Final weapons check, safeties off. We're hot, people. Stand by for the sound of my fire.
Out.

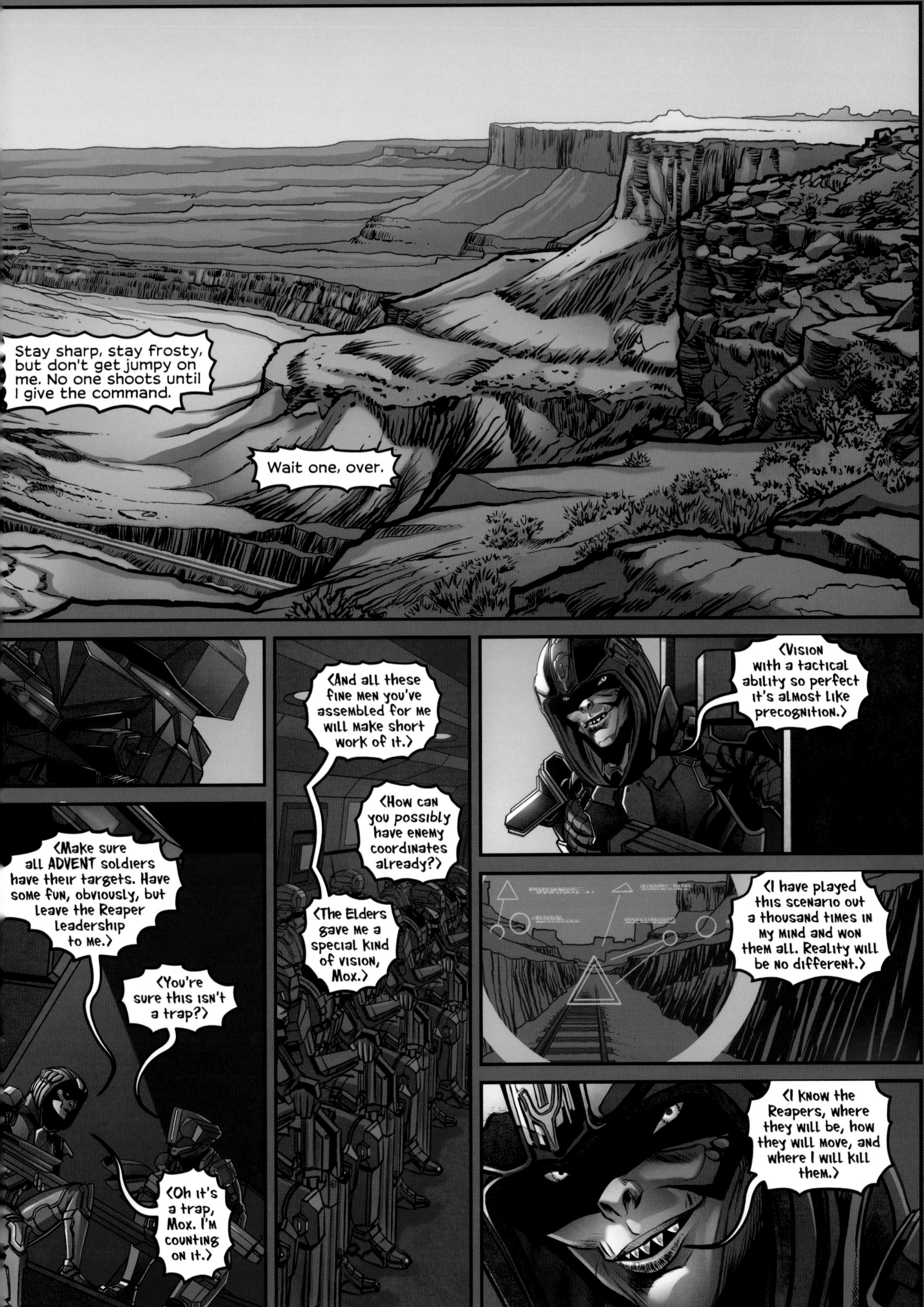
Stay sharp, stay frosty, but don't get jumpy on me. No one shoots until I give the command.
Wait one, over.
<Make sure all ADVENT soldiers have their targets. Have some fun, obviously, but leave the Reaper leadership to me.>
<You're sure this isn't a trap?>
<Oh it's a trap, Mox. I'm counting on it.>
<And all these fine men you've assembled for me will make short work of it.>
<How can you possibly have enemy coordinates already?>
<The Elders gave me a special kind of vision, Mox.>
<Vision with a tactical ability so perfect it's almost like precognition.>
<I have played this scenario out a thousand times in my mind and won them all. Reality will be no different.>
<I know the Reapers, where they will be, how they will move, and where I will kill them.>

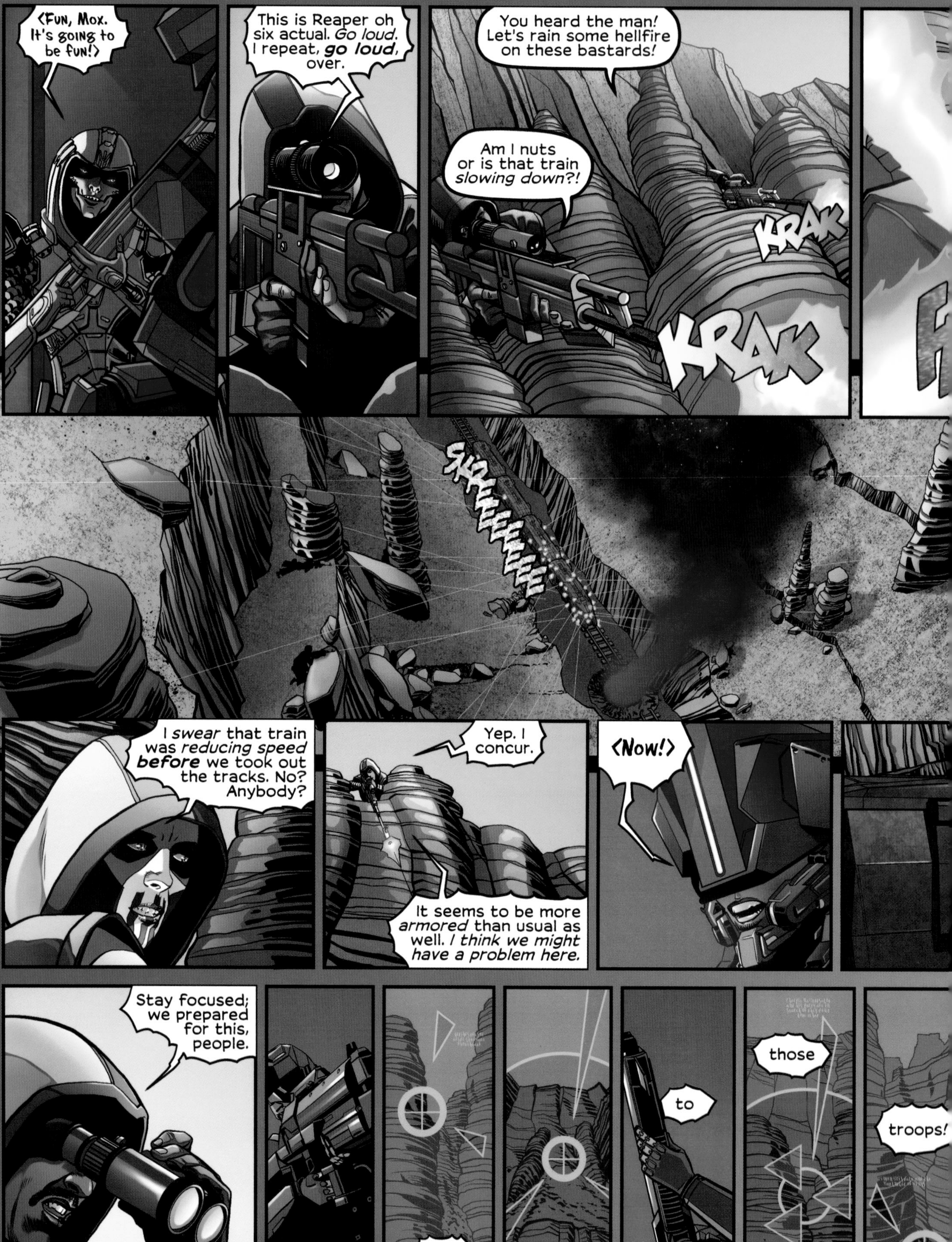
<Fun, Mox. It's going to be fun!>
This is Reaper oh six actual. *Go loud.* I repeat, ***go loud***, over.
You heard the man! Let's rain some hellfire on these bastards!
Am I nuts or is that train *slowing down*?!
KRAK
KRAK
I *swear* that train was *reducing speed* ***before*** we took out the tracks. No? Anybody?
Yep. I concur.
It seems to be more *armored* than usual as well. *I think we might have a problem here.*
<Now!>
Stay focused; we prepared for this, people.
Shift
your
fire
to
those
troops!

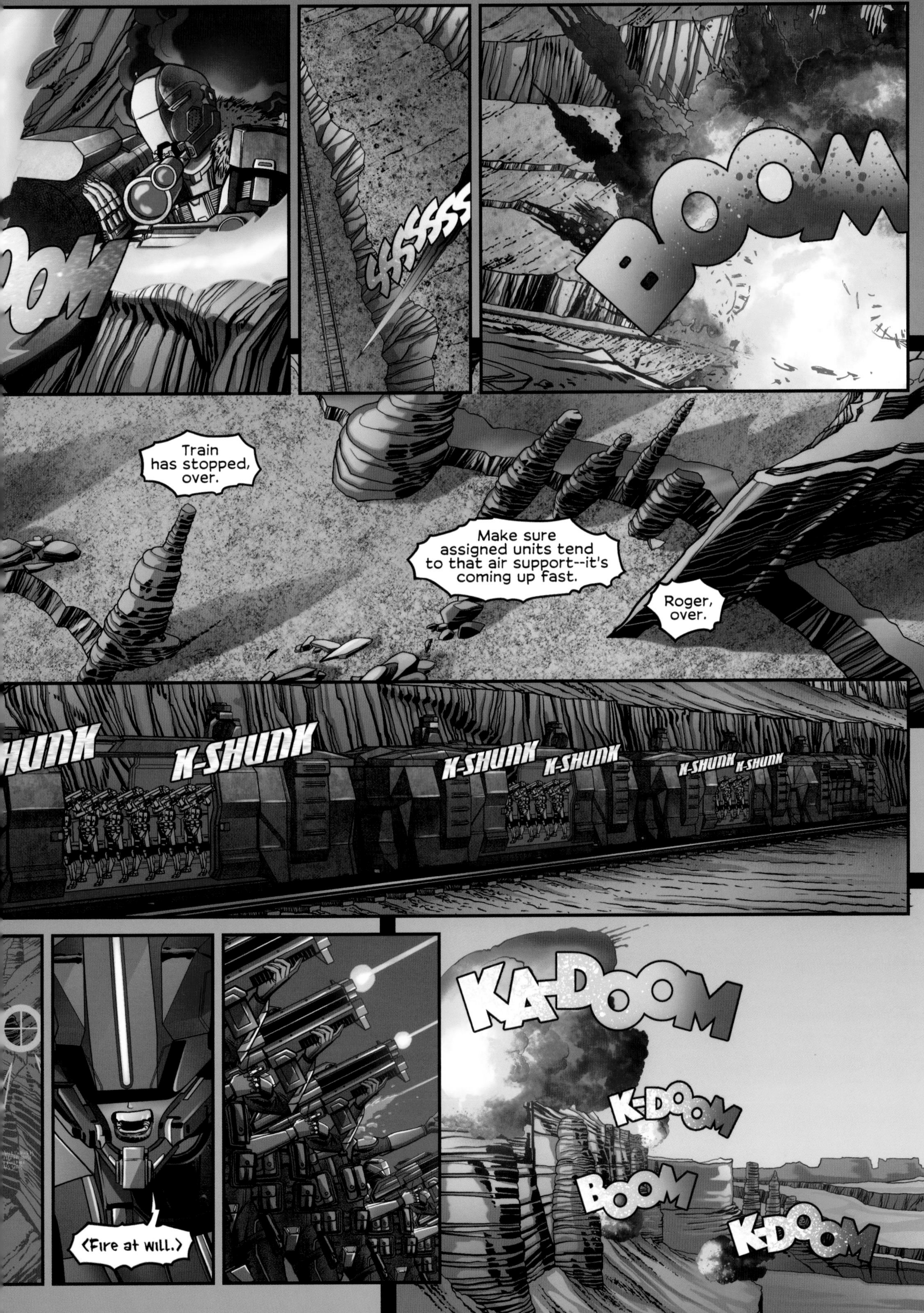

OOM
SSSSSSS
BOOM
Train has stopped, over.
Make sure assigned units tend to that air support--it's coming up fast.
Roger, over.
HUNK
K-SHUNK
K-SHUNK
K-SHUNK
K-SHUNK
K-SHUNK
<Fire at will.>
KA-DOOM
K-DOOM
BOOM
K-DOOM

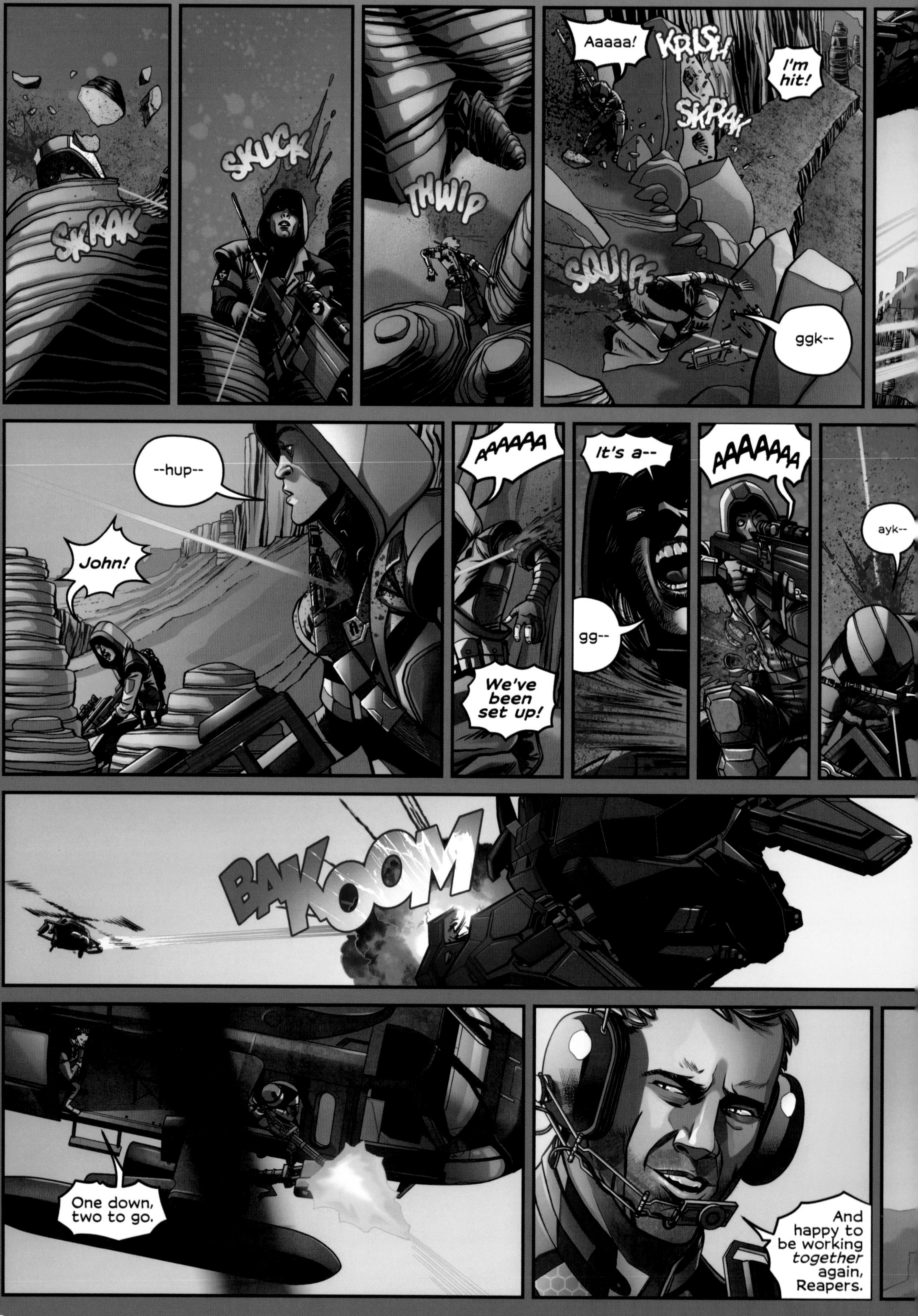
SKRAK
SKUCK
THWIP
Aaaaa!
KRISH
I'm hit!
SKRAK
SQUIFF
ggk--
--hup--
John!
AAAAAA
We've been set up!
It's a--
gg--
AAAAAAA
ayk--
BAKOOM
One down, two to go.
And happy to be working *together* again, Reapers.

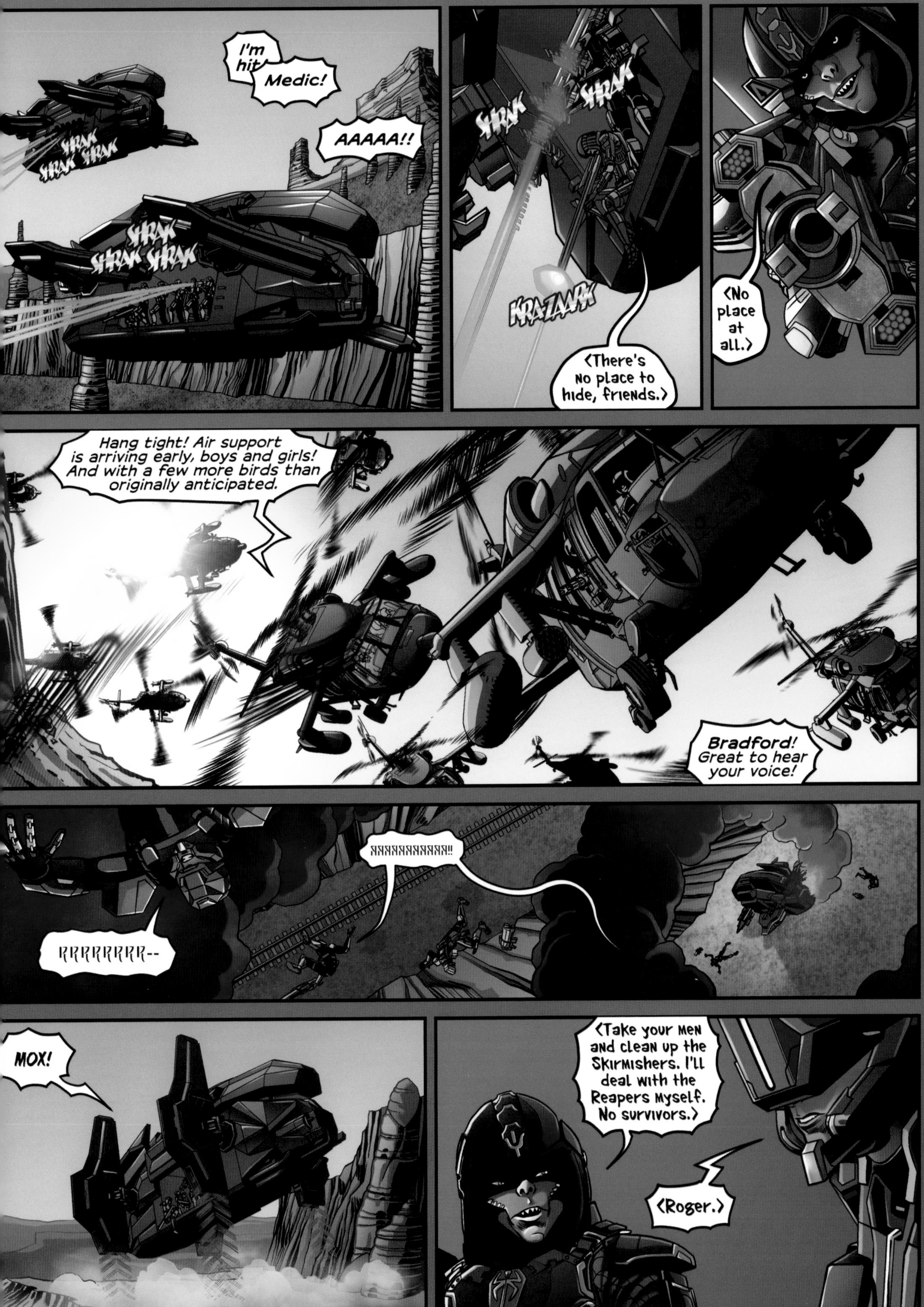

I'm hit
Medic!
SHRAK SHRAK SHRAK
AAAAA!!
SHRAK SHRAK SHRAK
SHRAK SHRAK
KRA-ZAARK
<There's no place to hide, friends.>
<No place at all.>
Hang tight! Air support is arriving early, boys and girls! And with a few more birds than originally anticipated.
Bradford! Great to hear your voice!
RRRRRRRR--
MOX!
<Take your men and clean up the Skirmishers. I'll deal with the Reapers myself. No survivors.>
<Roger.>

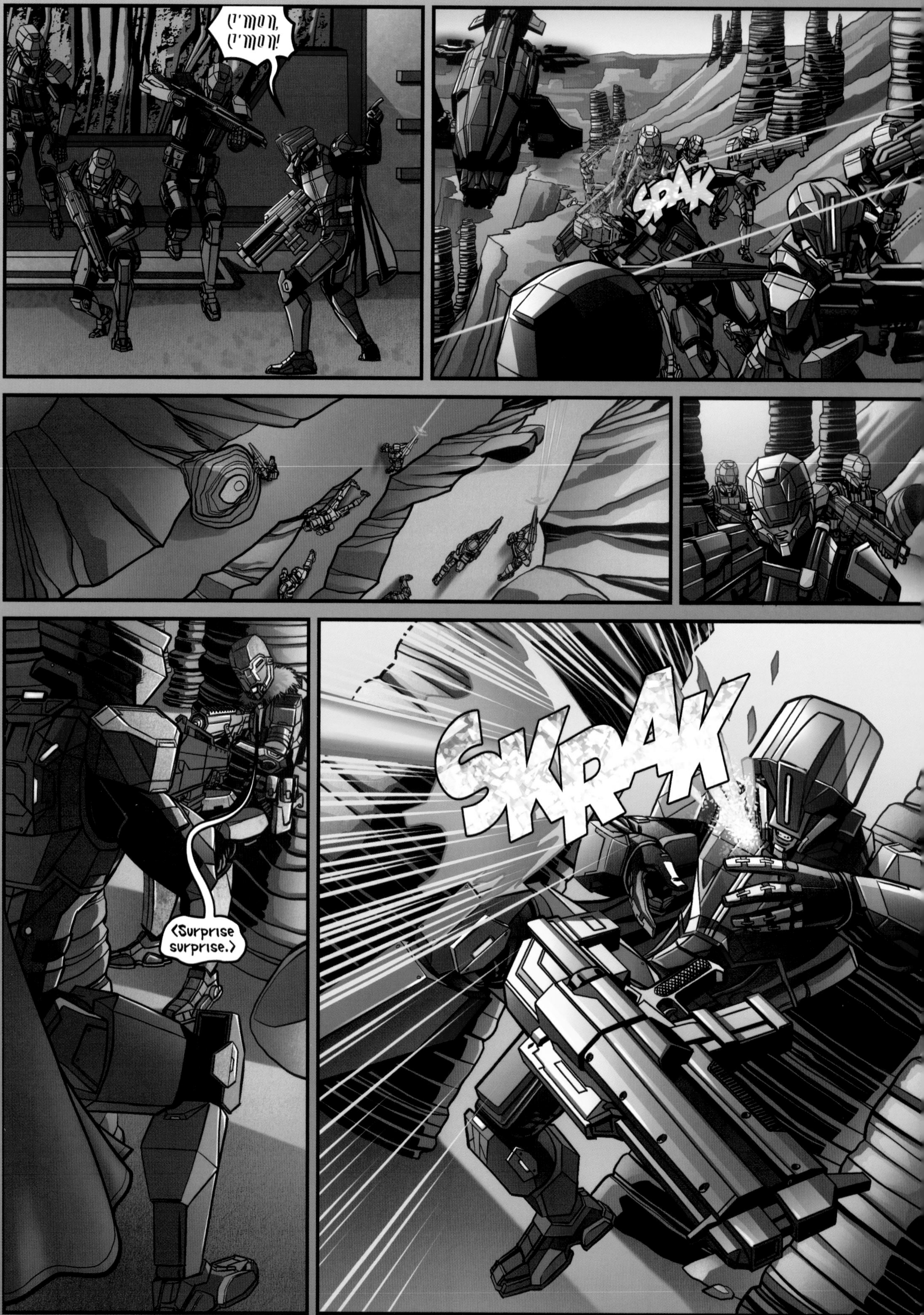
C'MON, C'MON!
SPAK
SKRAK
<Surprise surprise.>

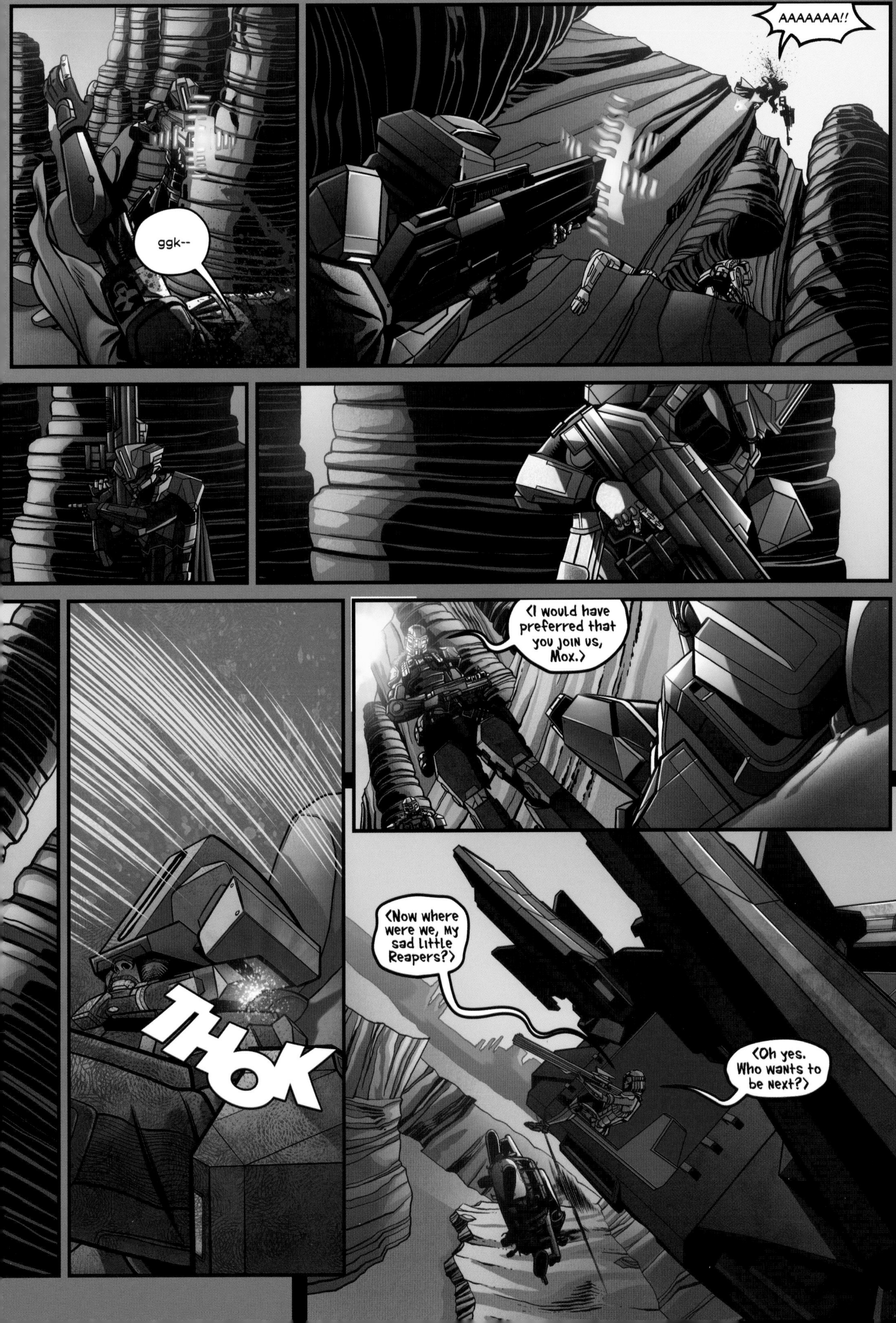
ggk--
AAAAAAA!!
THOK
<I would have preferred that you join us, Mox.>
<Now where were we, my sad little Reapers?>
<Oh yes. Who wants to be next?>

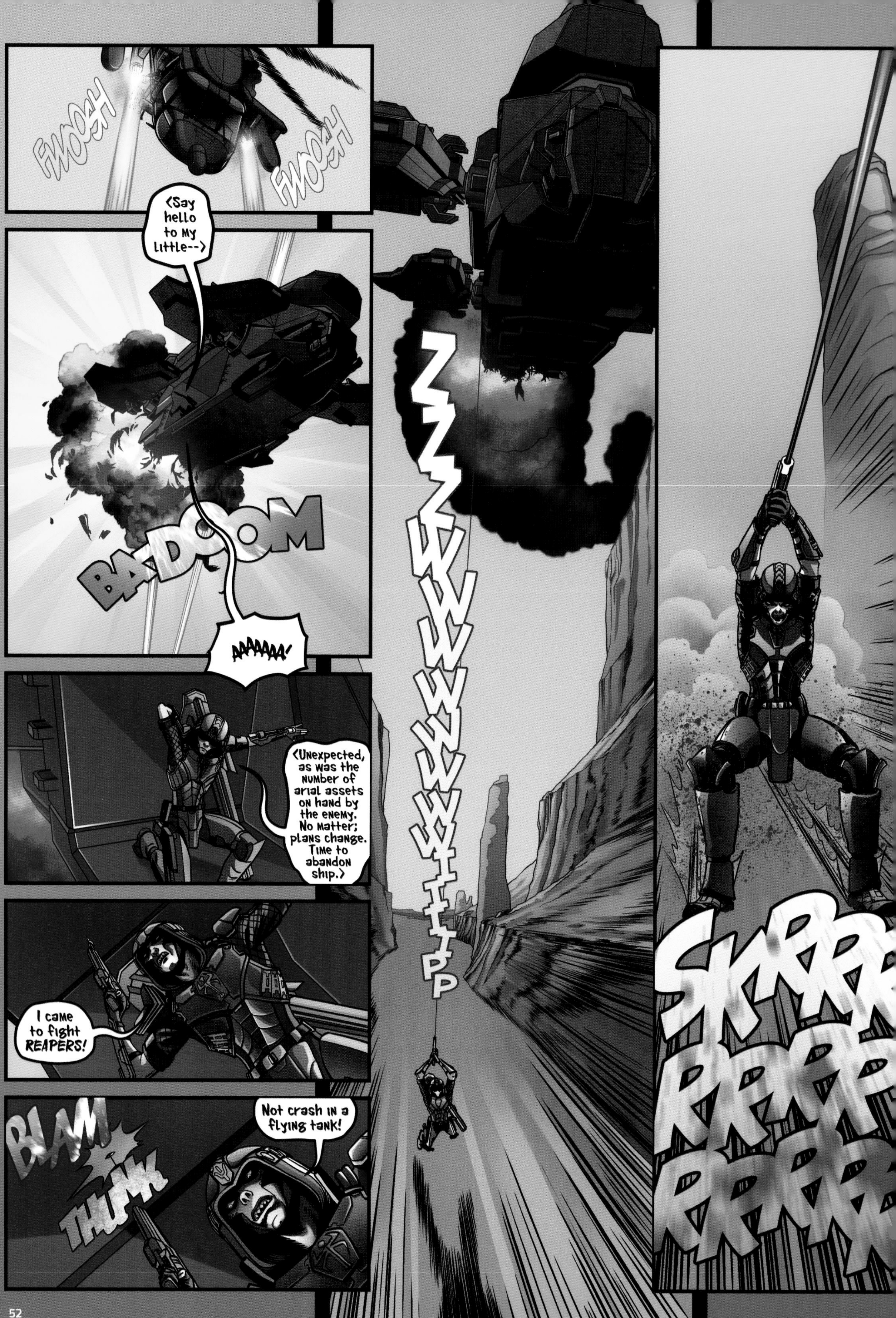
FWOOSH
FWOOSH
<Say hello to my little-->
BA-DOOM
AAAAAAA!
<Unexpected, as was the number of arial assets on hand by the enemy. No matter; plans change. Time to abandon ship.>
I came to fight REAPERS!
BLAM
THUNK
Not crash in a flying tank!
ZZZWWWWWWWWWIIIPP
SKRRRRRRRRRRRR

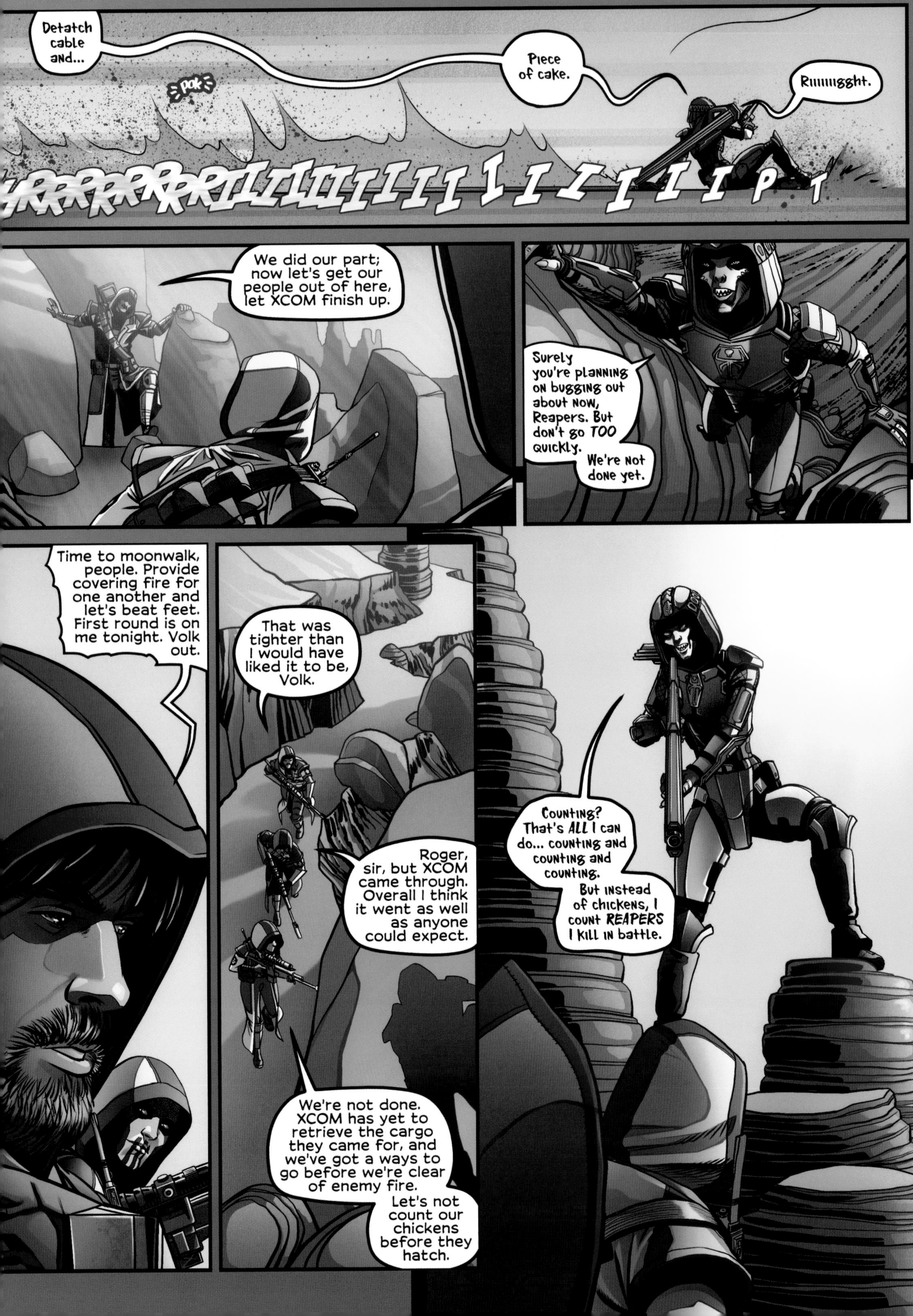
Detatch cable and...
POK
Piece of cake.
Riiiiiiiiggght.
We did our part; now let's get our people out of here, let XCOM finish up.
Surely you're planning on bugging out about now, Reapers. But don't go TOO quickly.
We're not done yet.
Time to moonwalk, people. Provide covering fire for one another and let's beat feet. First round is on me tonight. Volk out.
That was tighter than I would have liked it to be, Volk.
Roger, sir, but XCOM came through. Overall I think it went as well as anyone could expect.
We're not done. XCOM has yet to retrieve the cargo they came for, and we've got a ways to go before we're clear of enemy fire.
Let's not count our chickens before they hatch.
Counting? That's ALL I can do... counting and counting and counting.
But instead of chickens, I count REAPERS I kill in battle.

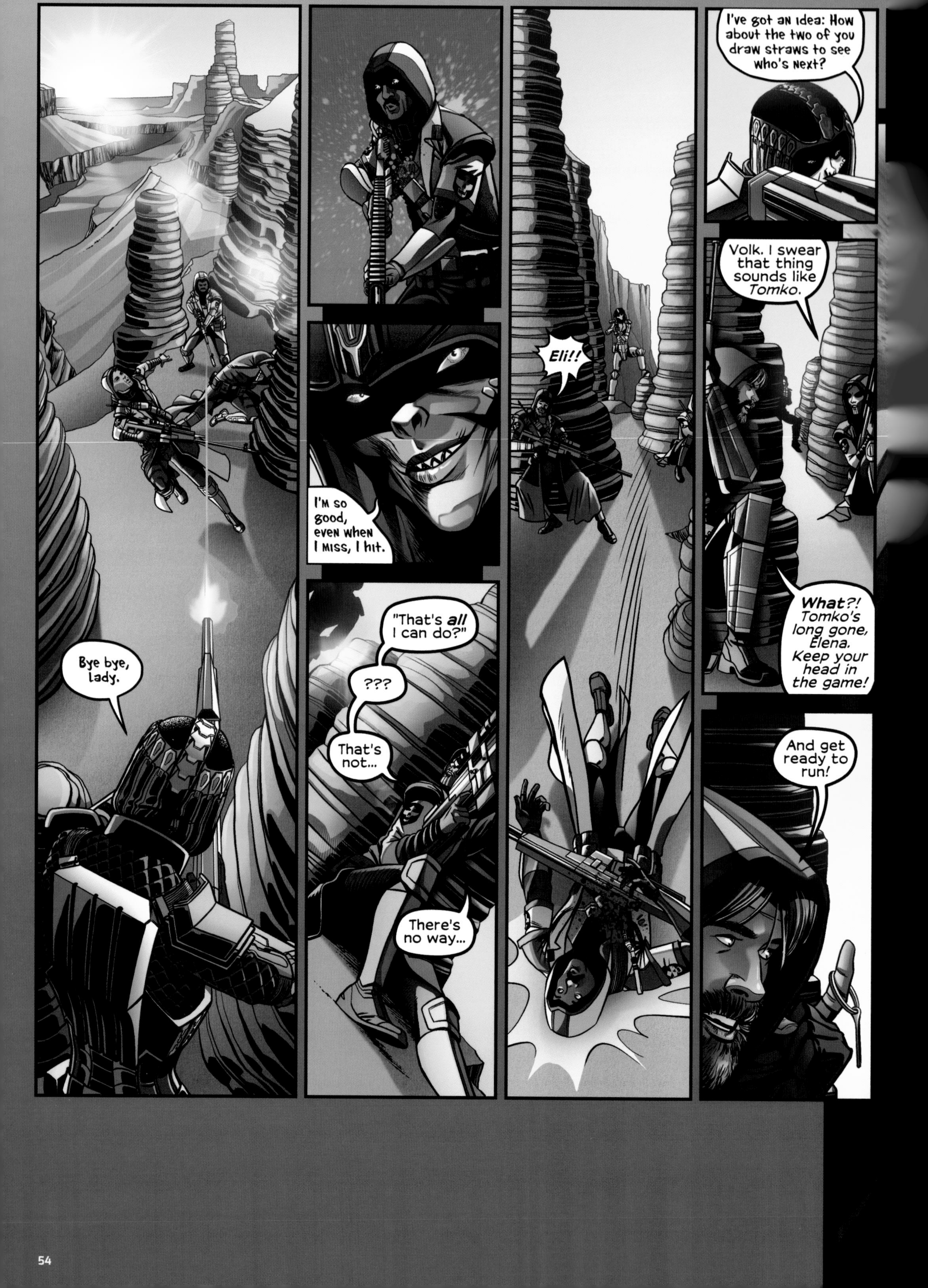
Bye bye, lady.
I'm so good, even when I miss, I hit.
"That's *all* I can do?"
???
That's not...
There's no way...
Eli!!
I've got an idea: How about the two of you draw straws to see who's next?
Volk. I swear that thing sounds like *Tomko*.
What?! *Tomko's long gone, Elena. Keep your head in the game!*
And get ready to run!

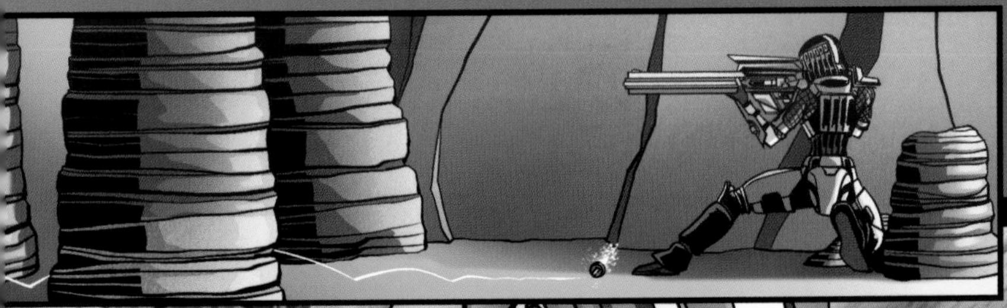

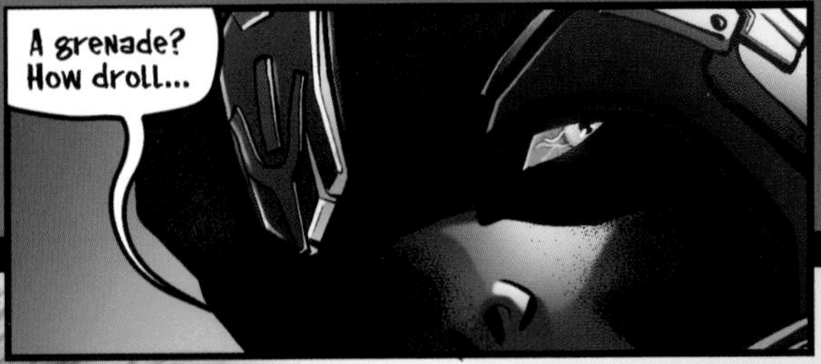
A grenade?
How droll...

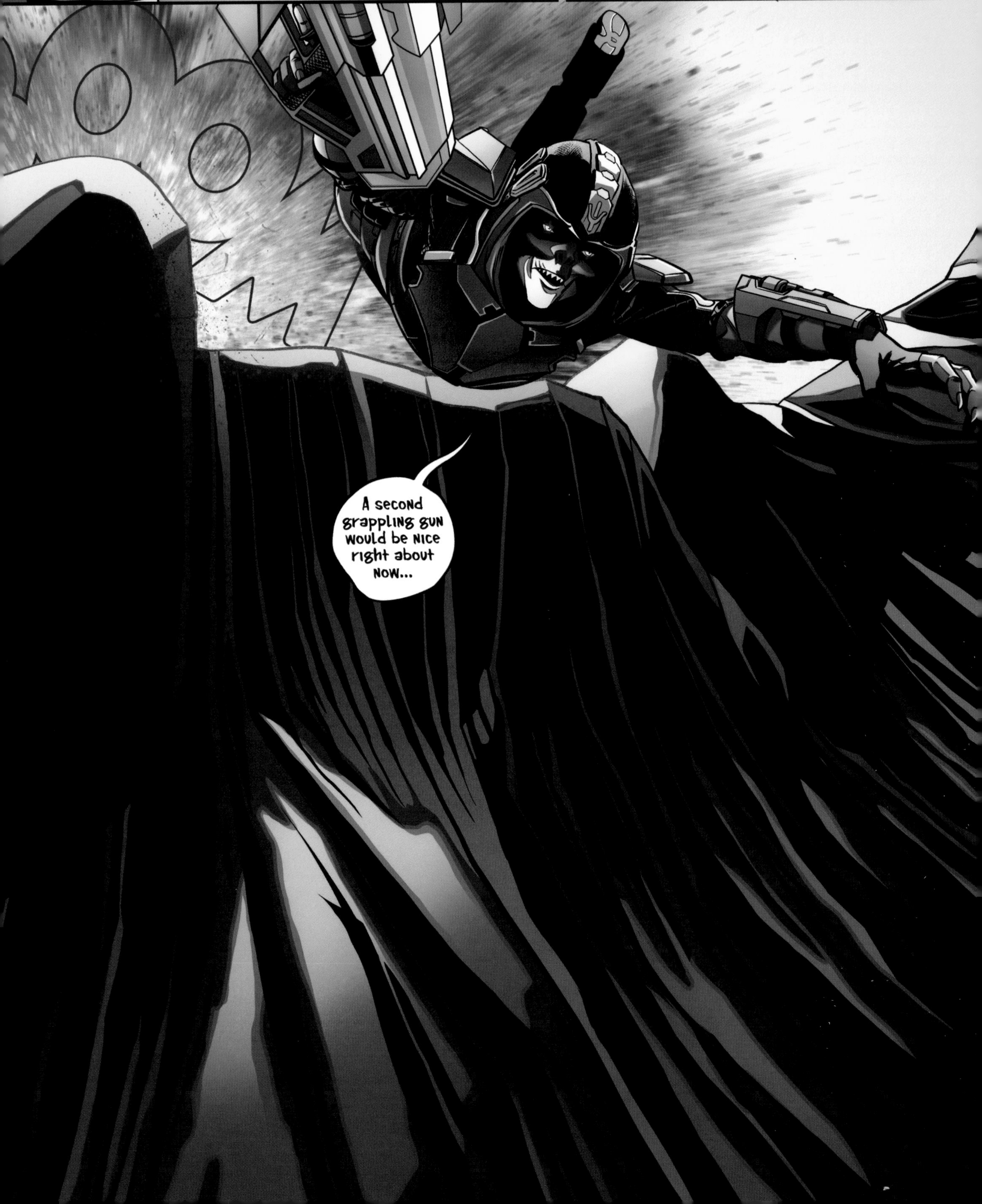
A second grappling gun would be nice right about now...

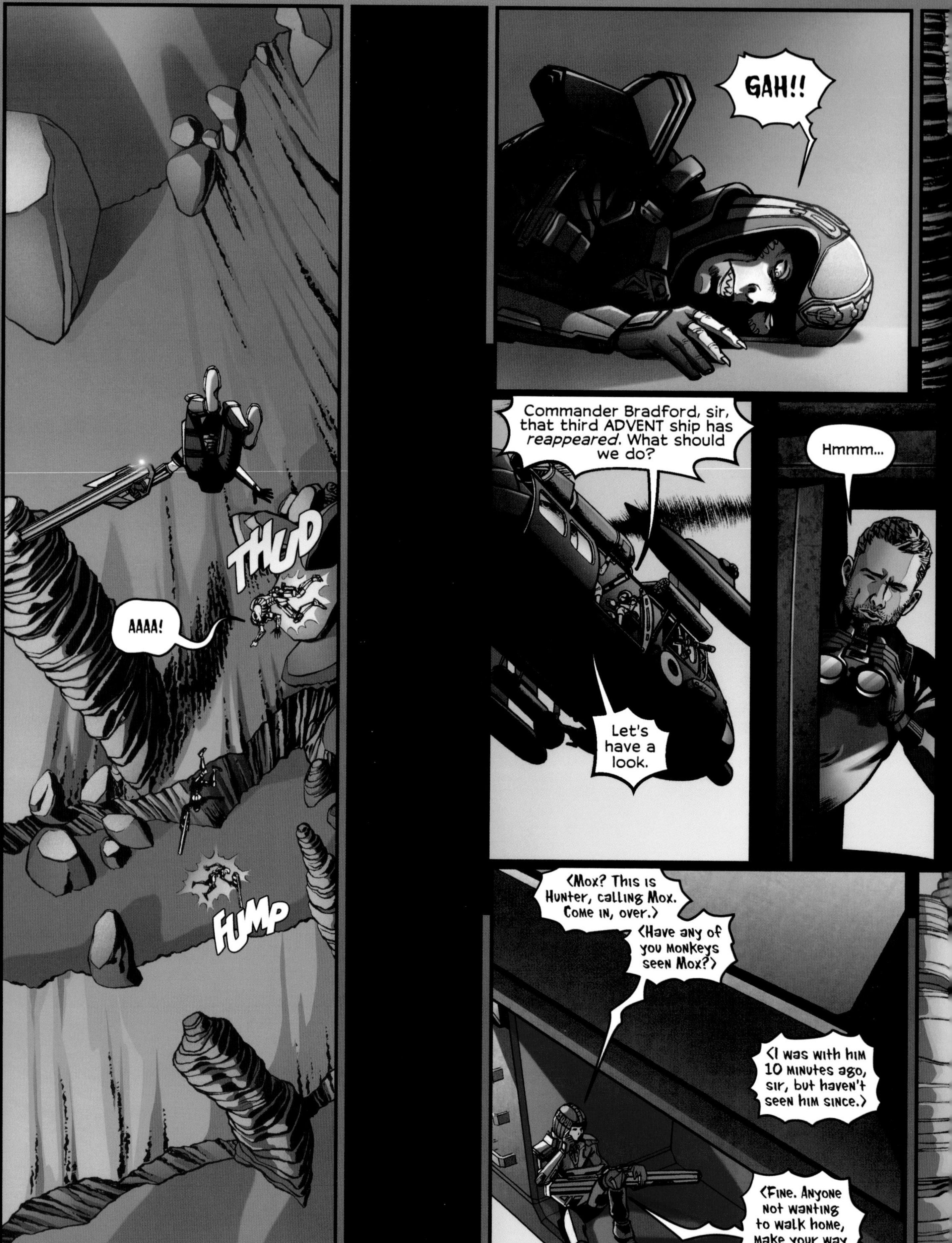
THUD
AAAA!
FUMP
GAH!!
Commander Bradford, sir, that third ADVENT ship has *reappeared*. What should we do?
Hmmm...
Let's have a look.
<Mox? This is Hunter, calling Mox. Come in, over.>
<Have any of you monkeys seen Mox?>
<I was with him 10 minutes ago, sir, but haven't seen him since.>
<Fine. Anyone not wanting to walk home, make your way to LZ Charlie. Get moving, over.>

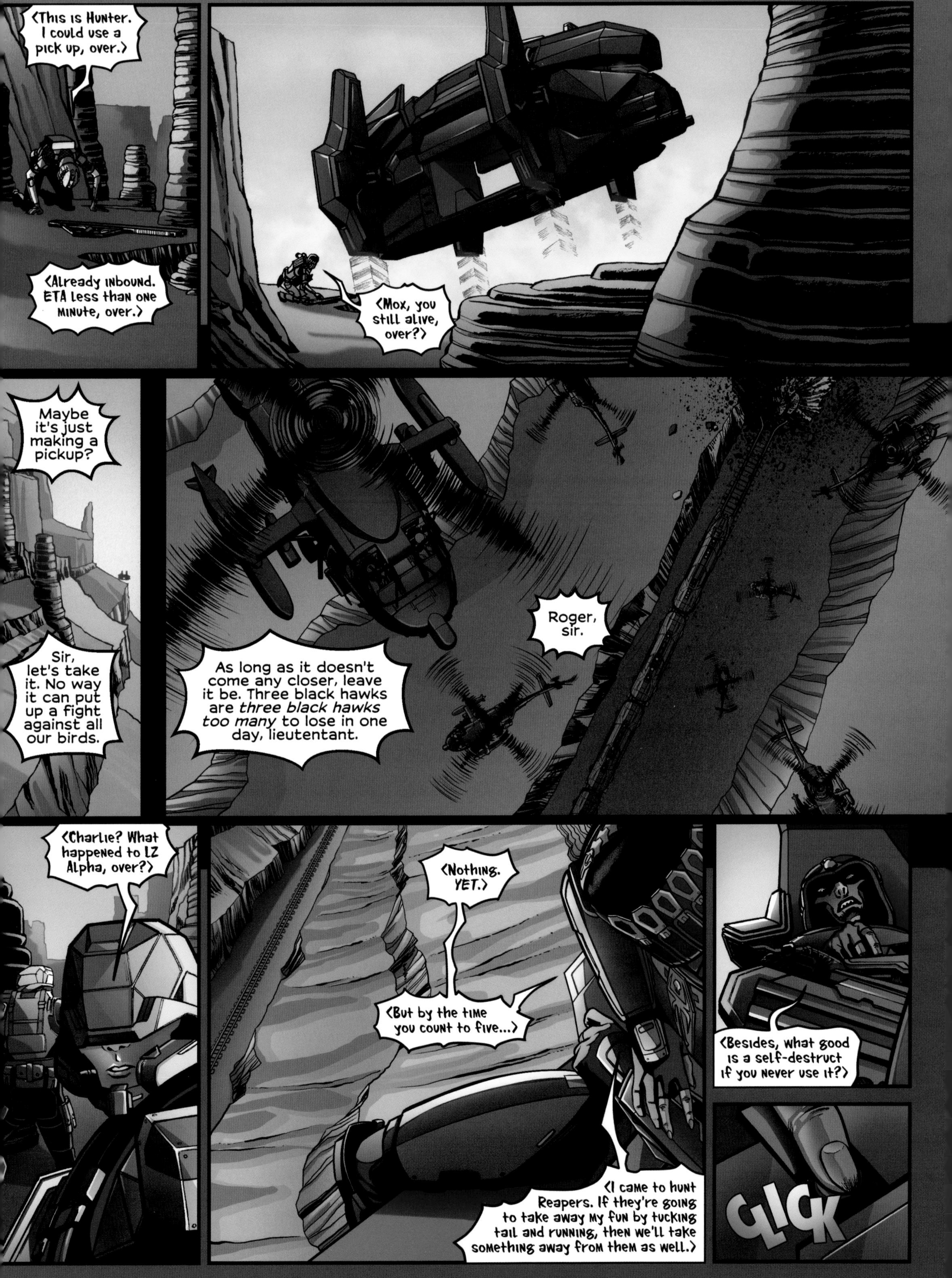

<This is Hunter. I could use a pick up, over.>
<Already inbound. ETA less than one minute, over.>
<Mox, you still alive, over?>
Maybe it's just making a pickup?
Sir, let's take it. No way it can put up a fight against all our birds.
As long as it doesn't come any closer, leave it be. Three black hawks are *three black hawks too many* to lose in one day, lieutentant.
Roger, sir.
<Charlie? What happened to LZ Alpha, over?>
<Nothing. YET.>
<But by the time you count to five...>
<I came to hunt Reapers. If they're going to take away my fun by tucking tail and running, then we'll take something away from them as well.>
<Besides, what good is a self-destruct if you never use it?>
CLICK

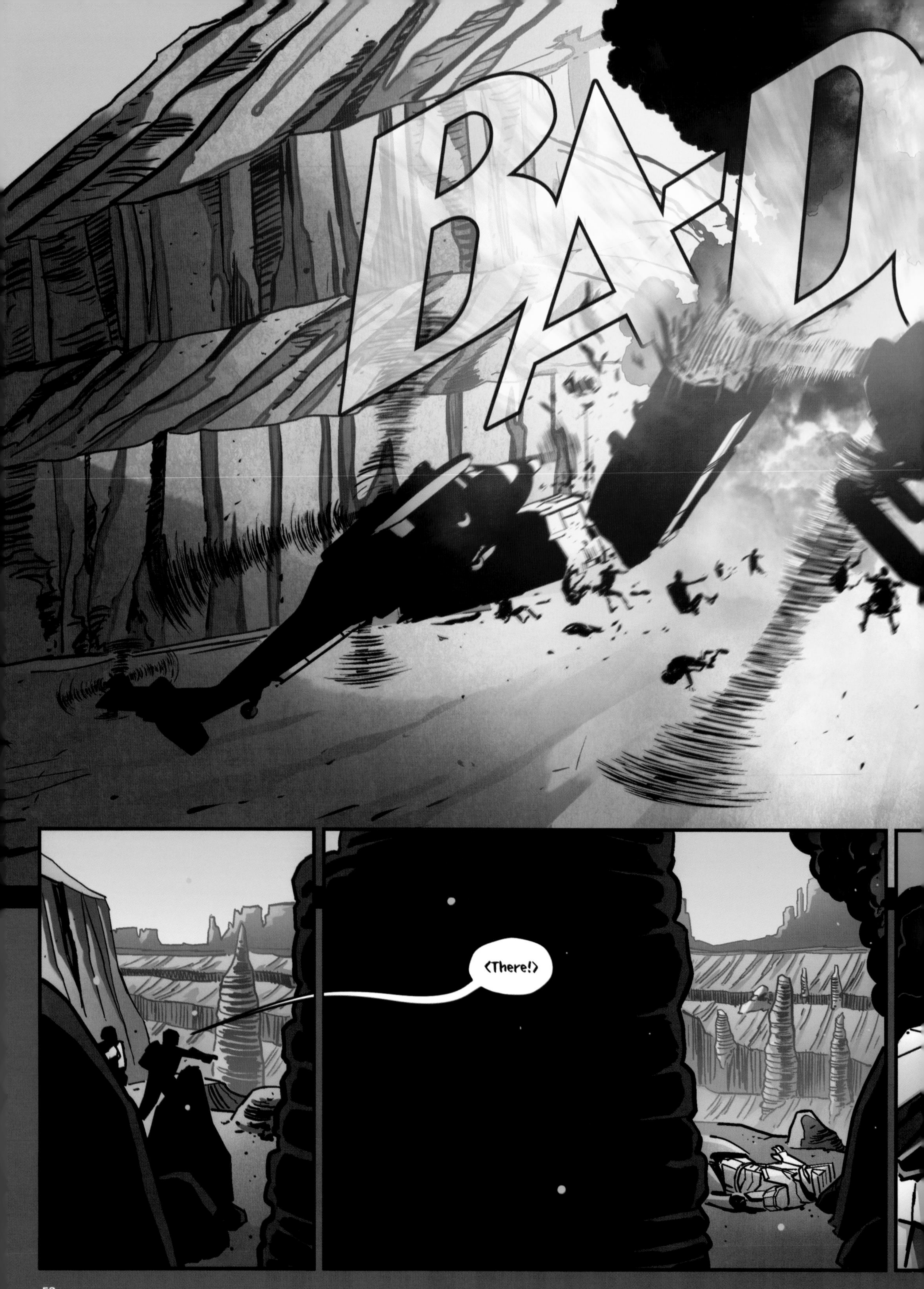
<There!>

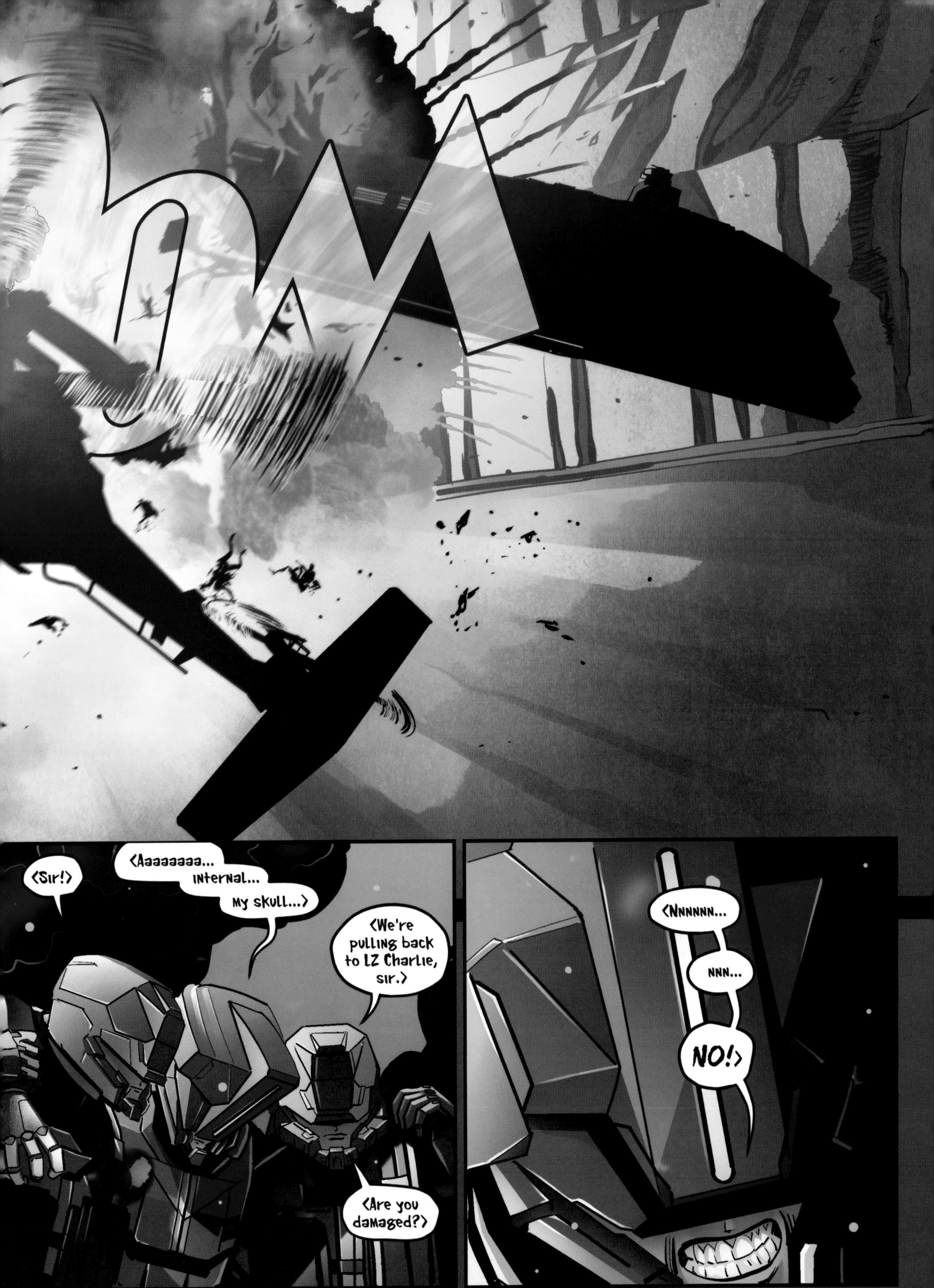

<Sir!>
<Aaaaaaaa... internal... my skull...>
<We're pulling back to LZ Charlie, sir.>
<Are you damaged?>
<Nnnnnn... nnn... NO!>

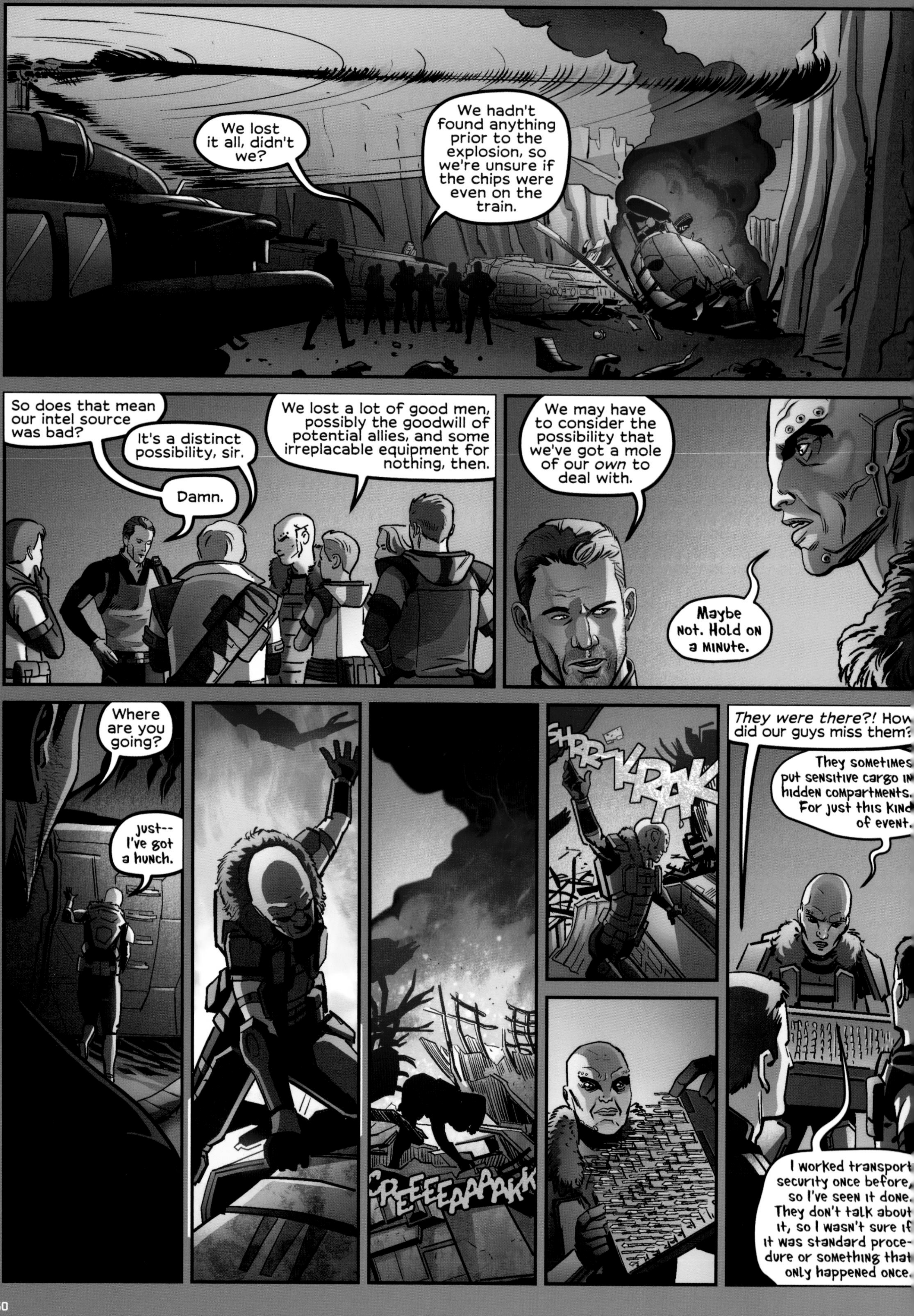

We lost it all, didn't we?
We hadn't found anything prior to the explosion, so we're unsure if the chips were even on the train.
So does that mean our intel source was bad?
It's a distinct possibility, sir.
Damn.
We lost a lot of good men, possibly the goodwill of potential allies, and some irreplacable equipment for nothing, then.
We may have to consider the possibility that we've got a mole of our *own* to deal with.
Maybe not. Hold on a minute.
Where are you going?
Just-- I've got a hunch.
CREEEEAAAAKK
SHRRKRAK
They were there?! How did our guys miss them?
They sometimes put sensitive cargo in hidden compartments. For just this kind of event.
I worked transport security once before, so I've seen it done. They don't talk about it, so I wasn't sure if it was standard procedure or something that only happened once.

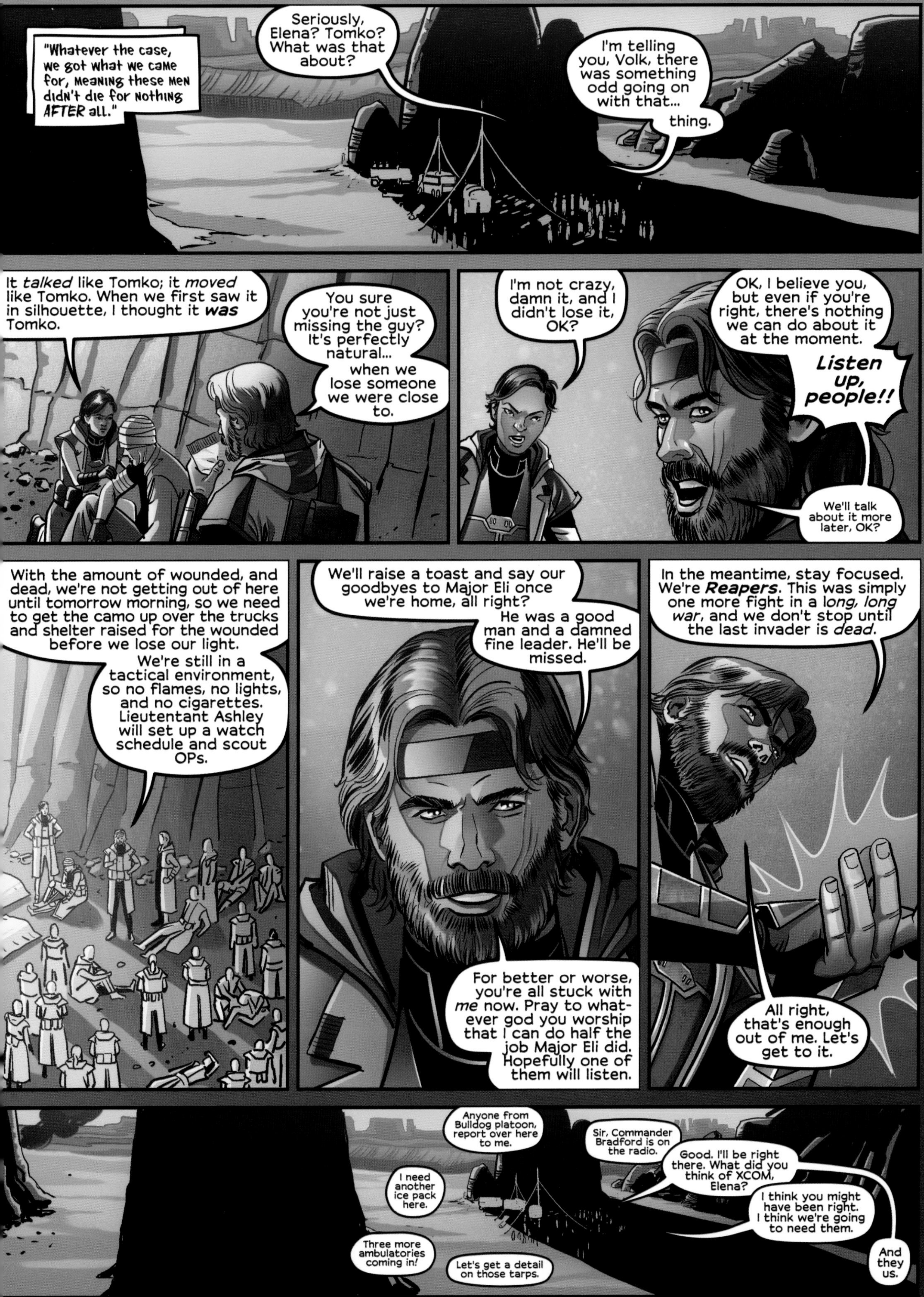
"Whatever the case, we got what we came for, meaning these men didn't die for nothing AFTER all."
Seriously, Elena? Tomko? What was that about?
I'm telling you, Volk, there was something odd going on with that...
thing.
It talked like Tomko; it moved like Tomko. When we first saw it in silhouette, I thought it was Tomko.
You sure you're not just missing the guy? It's perfectly natural...
when we lose someone we were close to.
I'm not crazy, damn it, and I didn't lose it, OK?
OK, I believe you, but even if you're right, there's nothing we can do about it at the moment.
Listen up, people!!
We'll talk about it more later, OK?
With the amount of wounded, and dead, we're not getting out of here until tomorrow morning, so we need to get the camo up over the trucks and shelter raised for the wounded before we lose our light.
We're still in a tactical environment, so no flames, no lights, and no cigarettes. Lieutentant Ashley will set up a watch schedule and scout OPs.
We'll raise a toast and say our goodbyes to Major Eli once we're home, all right?
He was a good man and a damned fine leader. He'll be missed.
For better or worse, you're all stuck with me now. Pray to whatever god you worship that I can do half the job Major Eli did. Hopefully one of them will listen.
In the meantime, stay focused. We're Reapers. This was simply one more fight in a long, long war, and we don't stop until the last invader is dead.
All right, that's enough out of me. Let's get to it.
Anyone from Bulldog platoon, report over here to me.
I need another ice pack here.
Three more ambulatories coming in!
Let's get a detail on those tarps.
Sir, Commander Bradford is on the radio.
Good. I'll be right there. What did you think of XCOM, Elena?
I think you might have been right. I think we're going to need them.
And they us.

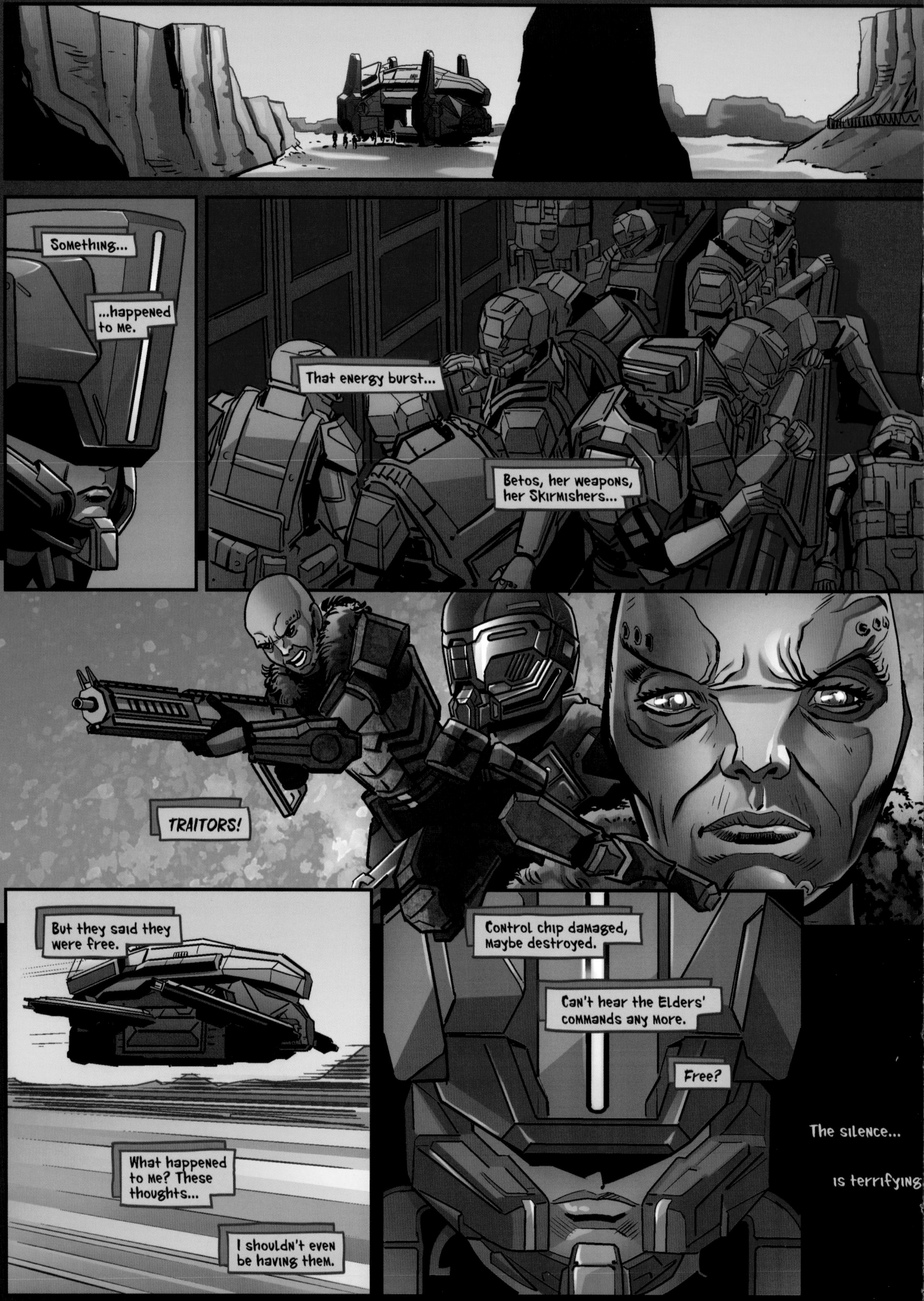
Something...
...happened to me.
That energy burst...
Betos, her weapons, her Skirmishers...
TRAITORS!
But they said they were free.
What happened to me? These thoughts...
I shouldn't even be having them.
Control chip damaged, maybe destroyed.
Can't hear the Elders' commands any more.
Free?
The silence...
is terrifying.

An Imprint of Insight Editions

PO Box 3088

San Rafael, CA

www.insightcomics.com

 Find us on Facebook: www.facebook.com/InsightEditionsComics

 Follow us on Twitter: @insightcomics

 Follow us on Instagram: Insight_Comics

Library of Congress Cataloging-in-Publication Data available.

ISBN: 978-1-60887-997-7

Publisher: Raoul Goff

Associate Publisher: Vanessa Lopez

Design Support: Evelyn Furuta

Executive Editor: Mark Irwin

Assistant Editor: Holly Fisher

Senior Production Editor: Elaine Ou

Production Manager: Sadie Crofts

ROOTS of PEACE   REPLANTED PAPER

Insight Editions, in association with Roots of Peace, will plant two trees for each tree used in the
manufacturing of this book. Roots of Peace is an internationally renowned humanitarian organization
dedicated to eradicating land mines worldwide and converting war-torn lands into productive farms
and wildlife habitats. Roots of Peace will plant two million fruit and nut trees in Afghanistan and provide
farmers there with the skills and support necessary for sustainable land use.

Manufactured in China by Insight Editions

10 9 8 7 6 5 4 3 2 1